Of Silver we have heard no more.
That formidable seafaring man with one leg
has at last gone clean out of my life;
but I dare say he met his old Negress,
and perhaps still lives in comfort with
her and Captain Flint. It is to be hoped so,
I suppose, for his chances of comfort in
another world are very small.

R.L. Stevenson, *Treasure Island*

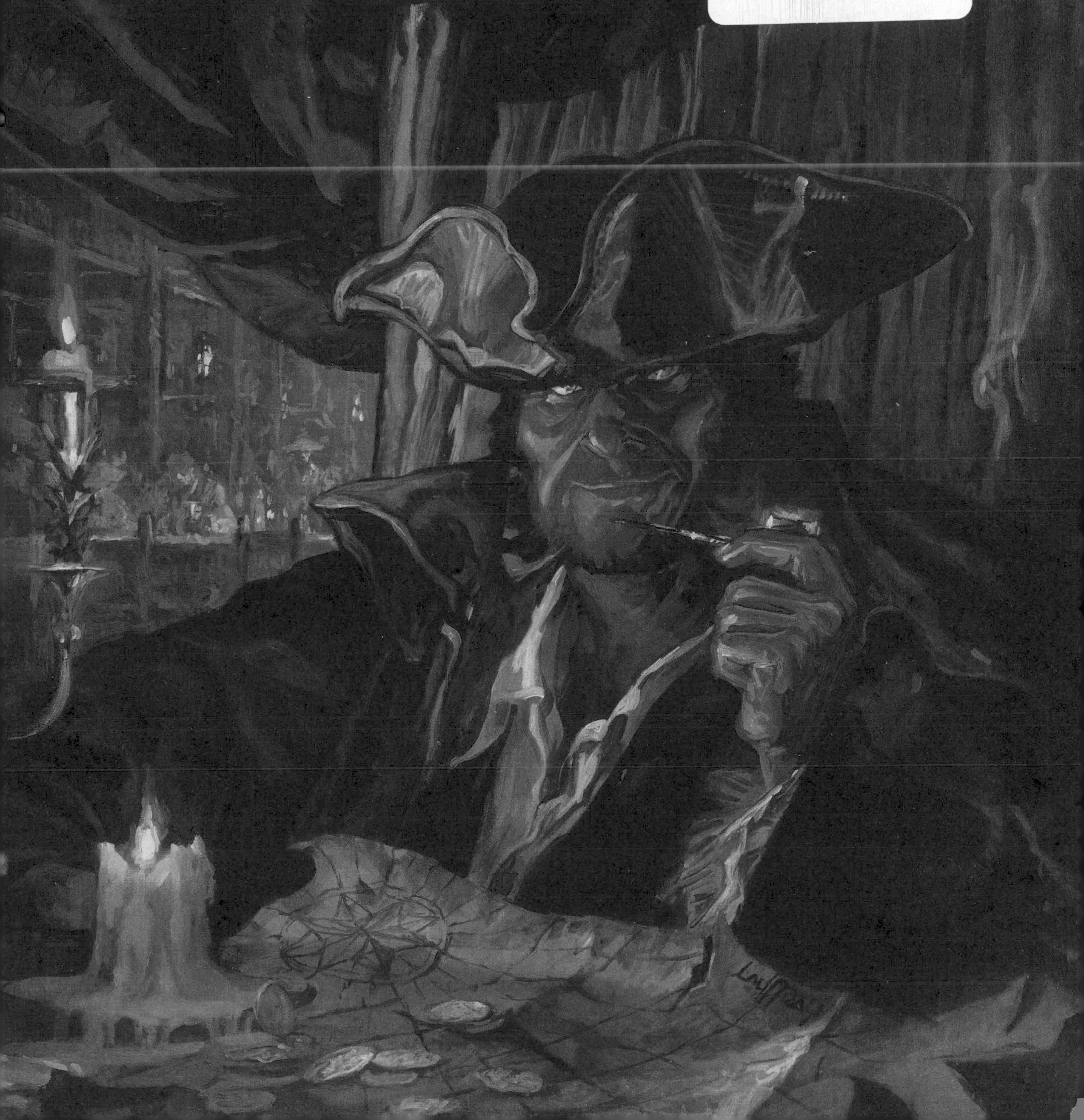

"ALIVE TODAY, DEAD TOMORROW,
WHAT DO WE CARE FOR LOOT AND HOARDS?
ALL THAT COUNTS IS THE DAY WE ARE LIVING,
AND NEVER THE ONE WE WILL HAVE TO LIVE…"

ALEXANDRE OEXMELIN
SURGEON TO THE BROTHERS OF THE COAST

THE STORY SO FAR…

DEEP INSIDE THE UNEXPLORED LANDS OF THE AMAZON, LORD BYRON HASTINGS HAS DISCOVERED THE CITY OF GUIANA-CAPAC AND ITS FABULOUS WEALTH. IN ORDER TO BRING THE TREASURE BACK TO ENGLAND, HE SENDS THE NATIVE MOXTECHICA WITH A LETTER ASKING HIS WIFE, LADY VIVIAN HASTINGS, TO FUND A SECOND EXPEDITION, AND HIS BROTHER, CAPTAIN EDWARD HASTINGS, TO LEAD IT.

WITH CHILD, VIVIAN KNOWS THAT HER HUSBAND WILL REPUDIATE HER—OR WORSE—ONCE HE DISCOVERS SHE IS PREGNANT.

SO, SHE CONVINCES DR LIVESEY TO HELP HER CONTACT PIRATE LONG JOHN SILVER AND HIS BROTHERS OF THE COAST SO SHE CAN MAKE A PACT WITH THEM. ALL WILL BOARD THE *NEPTUNE* WITH BUT A SINGLE GOAL: TO SEIZE THE INCAN TREASURE…

DURING THE CROSSING, THE SHIP'S CAPTAIN REALISES THAT HIS CREW HAS BEEN INFILTRATED BY THE PIRATES. LACKING PROOF, HE HAS A YOUNG SAILOR, JACK O'KIEF, CLAPPED IN IRONS. JACK IS SILVER'S PROTÉGÉ, HIRED INTO THE CREW BY A LOWLIFE NAMED PARIS AGAINST THE PIRATE'S OPPOSITION.

WITH VIVIAN'S HELP, SILVER MANAGES TO GO TO JACK. BUT IT'S TOO LATE. THE YOUNG MAN HAS SUCCUMBED TO THE FLOGGING ORDERED BY HASTINGS.

MAD WITH FURY, SILVER TRIGGERS A MUTINY.
DURING THE BATTLE, VIVIAN IS ASSAULTED BY TWO MUTINEERS. SHE ESCAPES THEM WITH LIVESEY'S HELP. LIKE HER, THE DOCTOR FINDS HIMSELF FORCED TO KILL TO SURVIVE.

LONG JOHN FIGHTS THE CAPTAIN AND KILLS HIM. IN THE RED HAZE OF HIS RAGE, HE THROWS THE BODY INTO THE OCEAN, ALONG WITH THE MAP TO GUIANA-CAPAC.

SAILORS AND PIRATES ARE NOW FREE, BUT COMPLETELY LOST AS THEY APPROACH THE MYSTERIOUS SHORES THAT HERALD IT AT LAST… THE NEW WORLD.

Original title: Long John Silver III – Le labyrinthe d'émeraude
Original edition: © Dargaud Paris, 2010 by Dorison & Lauffray
www.dargaud.com - All rights reserved
English translation: © 2011 Cinebook Ltd
Translator: Jerome Saincantin
Lettering and text layout: Imadjinn
Printed in Spain by Just Colour Graphic
This edition first published in Great Britain in 2011 by
Cinebook Ltd - 56 Beech Avenue
Canterbury, Kent - CT4 7TA
www.cinebook.com
A CIP catalogue record for this book
is available from the British Library
ISBN 978-1-84918-105-1

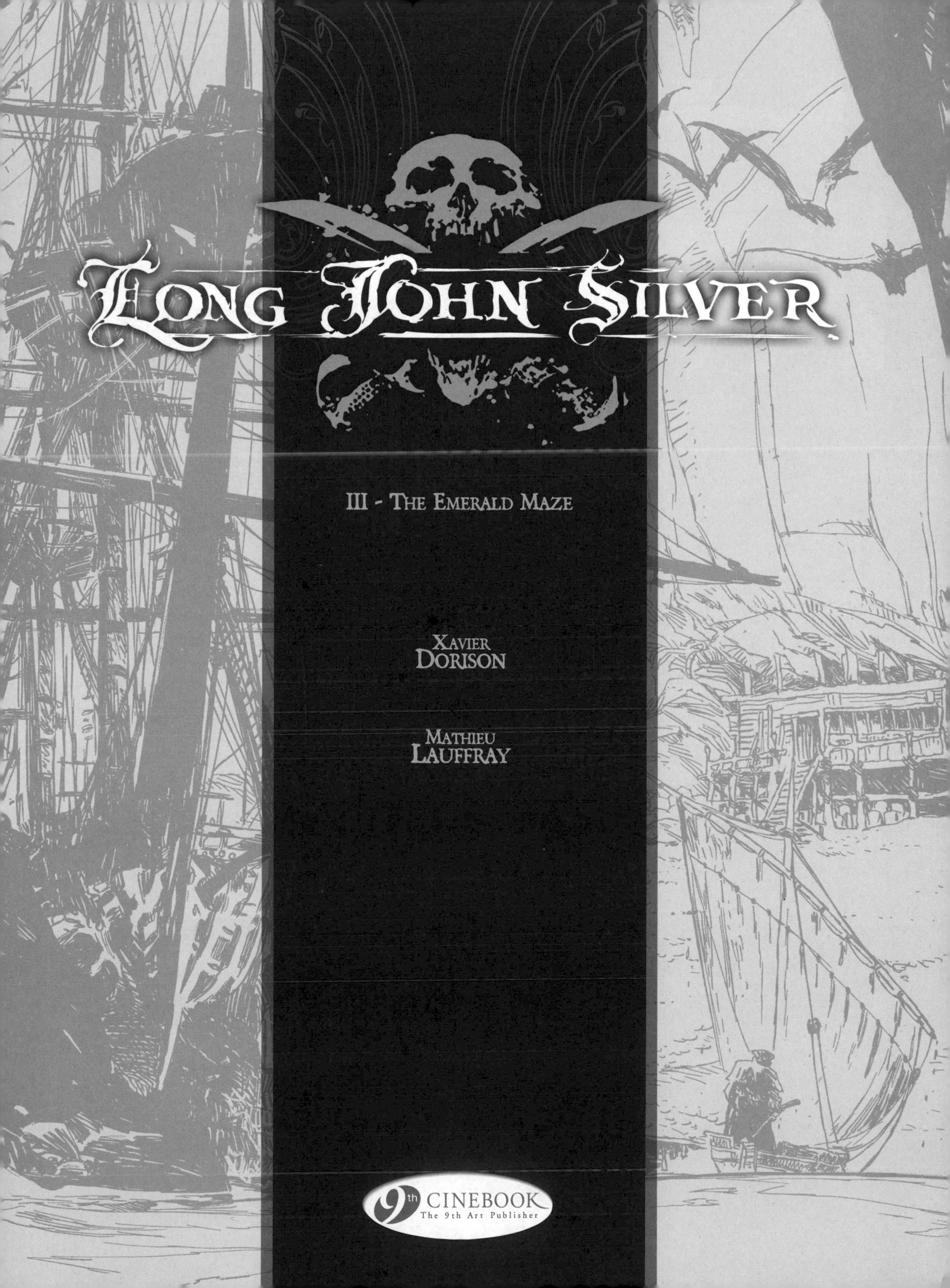

Long John Silver

III - The Emerald Maze

Xavier Dorison

Mathieu Lauffray

9th Cinebook
The 9th Art Publisher

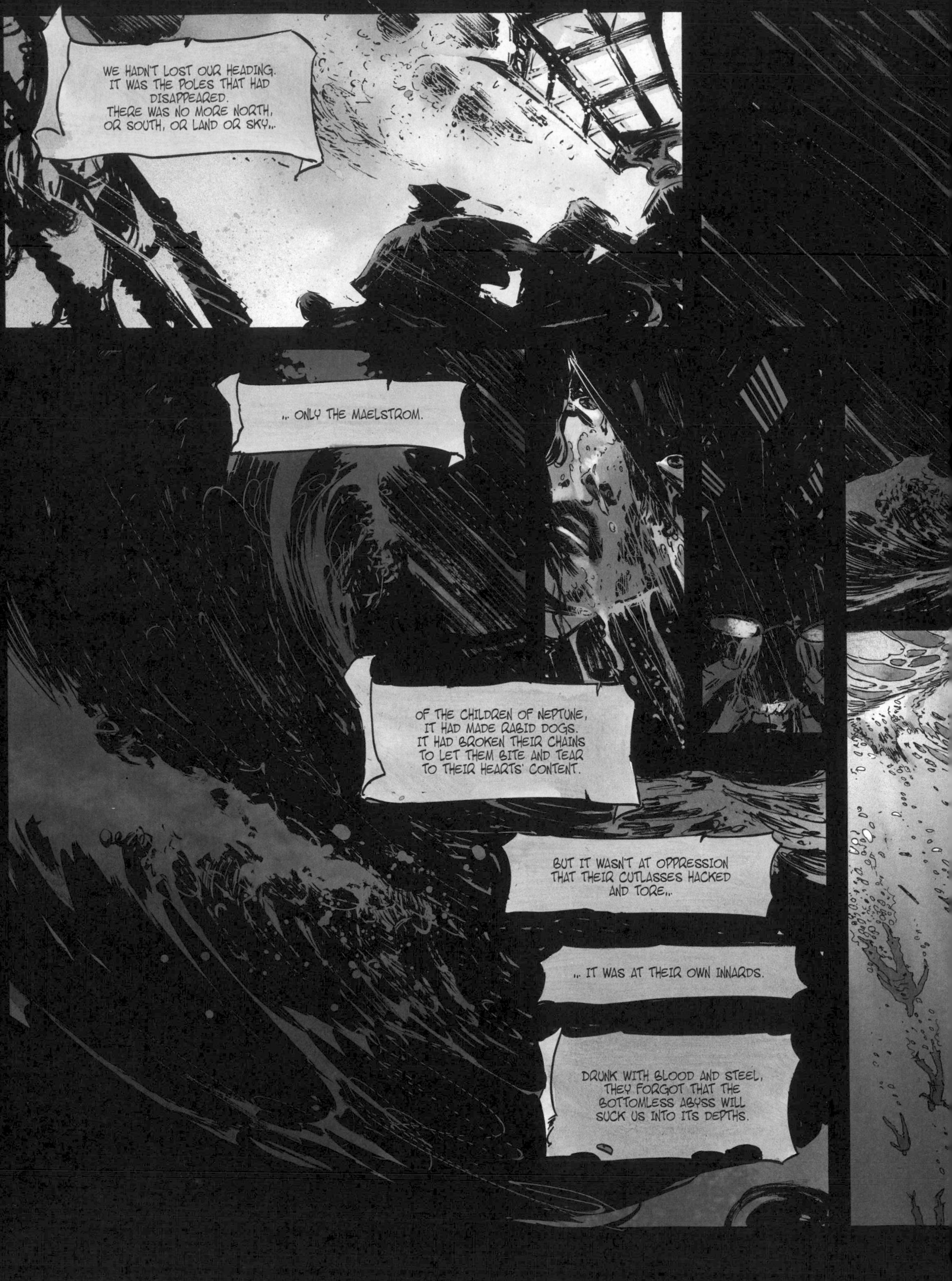
WE HADN'T LOST OUR HEADING. IT WAS THE POLES THAT HAD DISAPPEARED. THERE WAS NO MORE NORTH, OR SOUTH, OR LAND OR SKY...
... ONLY THE MAELSTROM.
OF THE CHILDREN OF NEPTUNE, IT HAD MADE RABID DOGS. IT HAD BROKEN THEIR CHAINS TO LET THEM BITE AND TEAR TO THEIR HEARTS' CONTENT.
BUT IT WASN'T AT OPPRESSION THAT THEIR CUTLASSES HACKED AND TORE...
... IT WAS AT THEIR OWN INNARDS.
DRUNK WITH BLOOD AND STEEL, THEY FORGOT THAT THE BOTTOMLESS ABYSS WILL SUCK US INTO ITS DEPTHS.

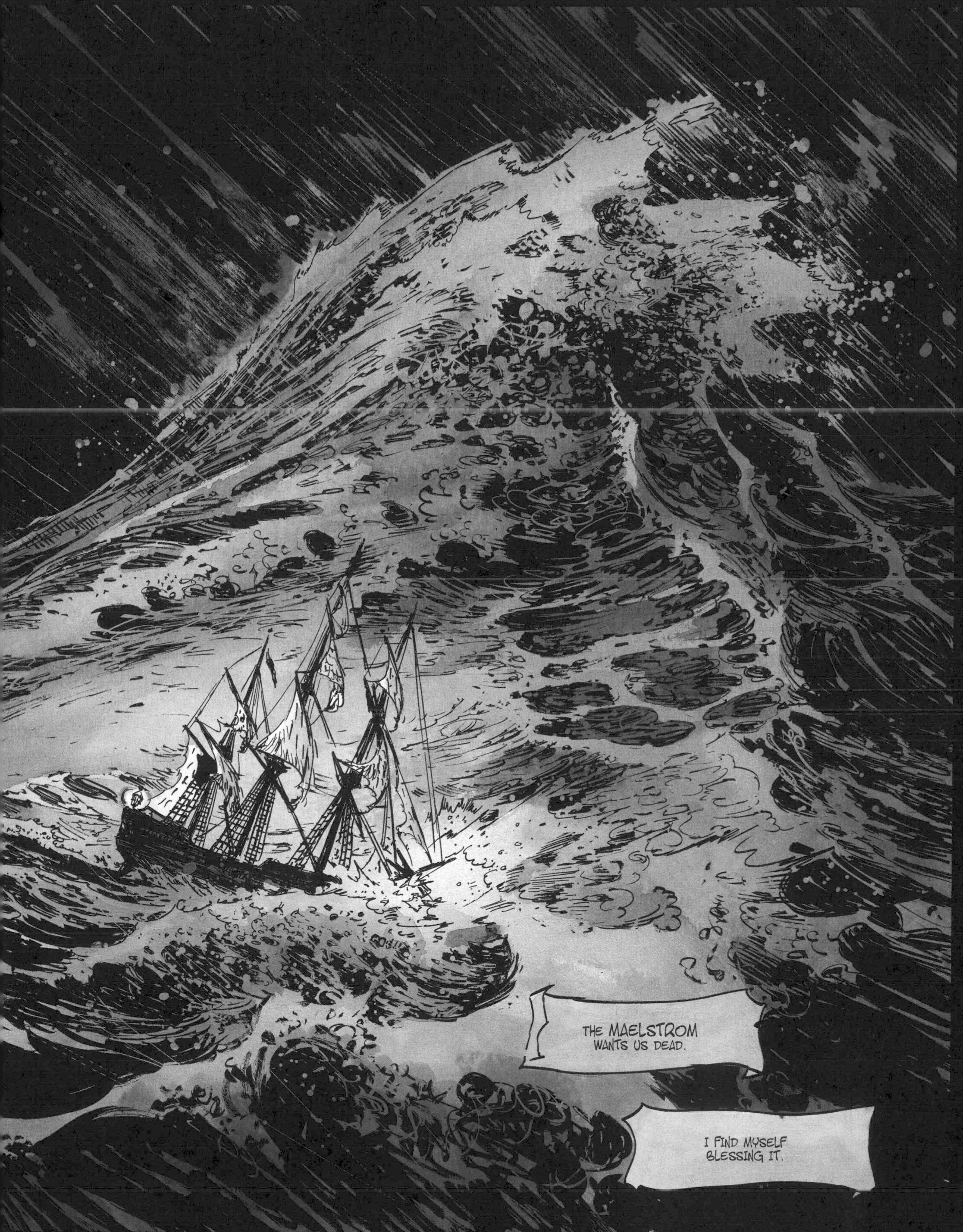
THE MAELSTROM WANTS US DEAD.
I FIND MYSELF BLESSING IT.

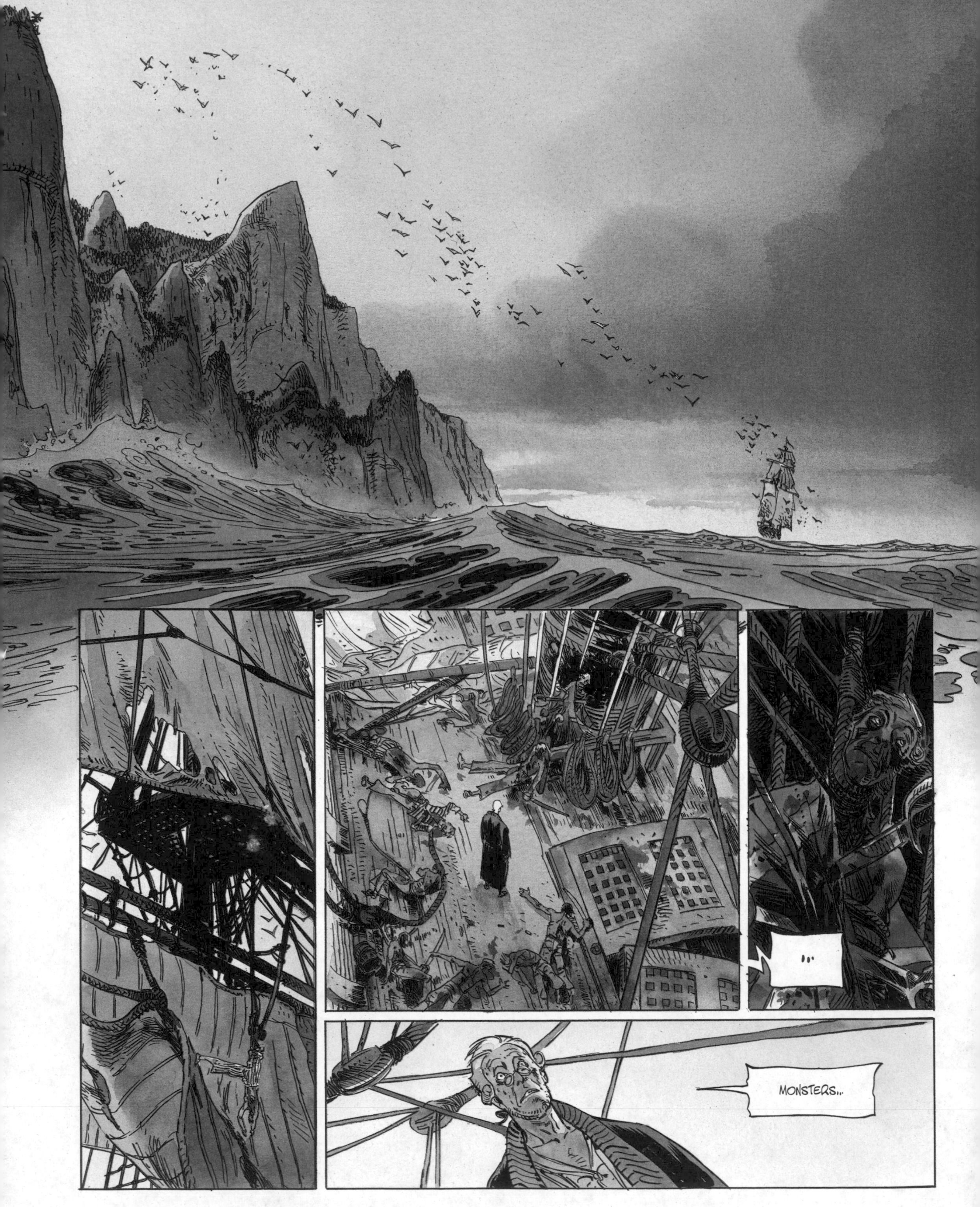
...
MONSTERS...

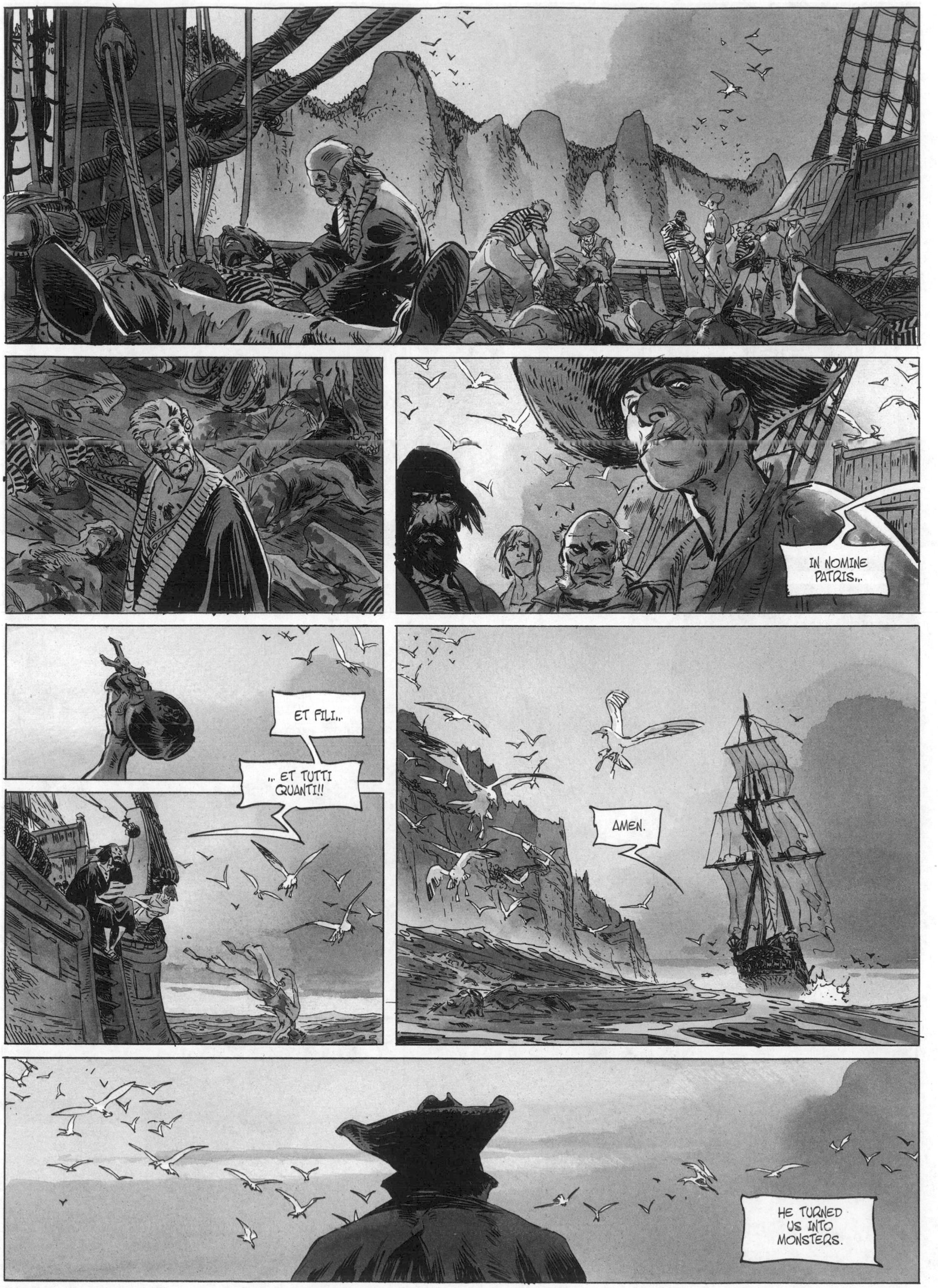
IN NOMINE PATRIS...
ET FILI...
... ET TUTTI QUANTI!!
AMEN.
HE TURNED US INTO MONSTERS.

CLANG! CLANG! CLANG!

PFFFF... WE'RE WASTING OUR TIME. THIS'LL NEVER HOLD!

IT WON'T DO, LONG JOHN. THIS BLASTED COCKLESHELL SPLIT OPEN LIKE AN OVERRIPE MELON. WE DON'T HAVE A PRAYER OF REPAIRING IT HERE.

WE HAVE TO GO ASHORE.

LOWER YOUR VOICE, YOU OLD TOAD. THE DECKS HAVE EARS.

GO ASHORE? IN THOSE REEFS? WE MIGHT AS WELL SCUTTLE HER NOW! BUT I'M SURE THE MOUTH OF THE AMAZON ISN'T FAR. HASTINGS SET A COURSE FOR IT.

WE MAY HAVE VEERED OFF COURSE DURING THE NIGHT, BUT NOT BY MORE THAN A FEW MILES... I'LL FIND A PASSAGE.

WELL, THEN, FIND IT QUICKLY, CAPTAIN. 'CAUSE WE'RE SINKING!

FREE DANTZIG. TAKE HIM WITH YOU TO THE HOLD.

DANTZIG? THAT BERIBBONED BASTARD OF AN OFFICER? WHAT USE COULD I HAVE FOR HIM? NOT TO MENTION THAT WITH THE BEATING WE GAVE HIM, HE'S BOUND TO HAVE GONE ALOFT!

YOU'D BETTER PRAY HE'S STILL ALIVE, OLAF! OFFICERS LIKE HIM LEARN TO CAULK A BOARD BEFORE THEY CAN WALK!! SO WIPE THAT AFFRONTED-MAIDEN EXPRESSION OFF YOUR FACE AND PUT HIM TO WORK TOOT SWEET!!

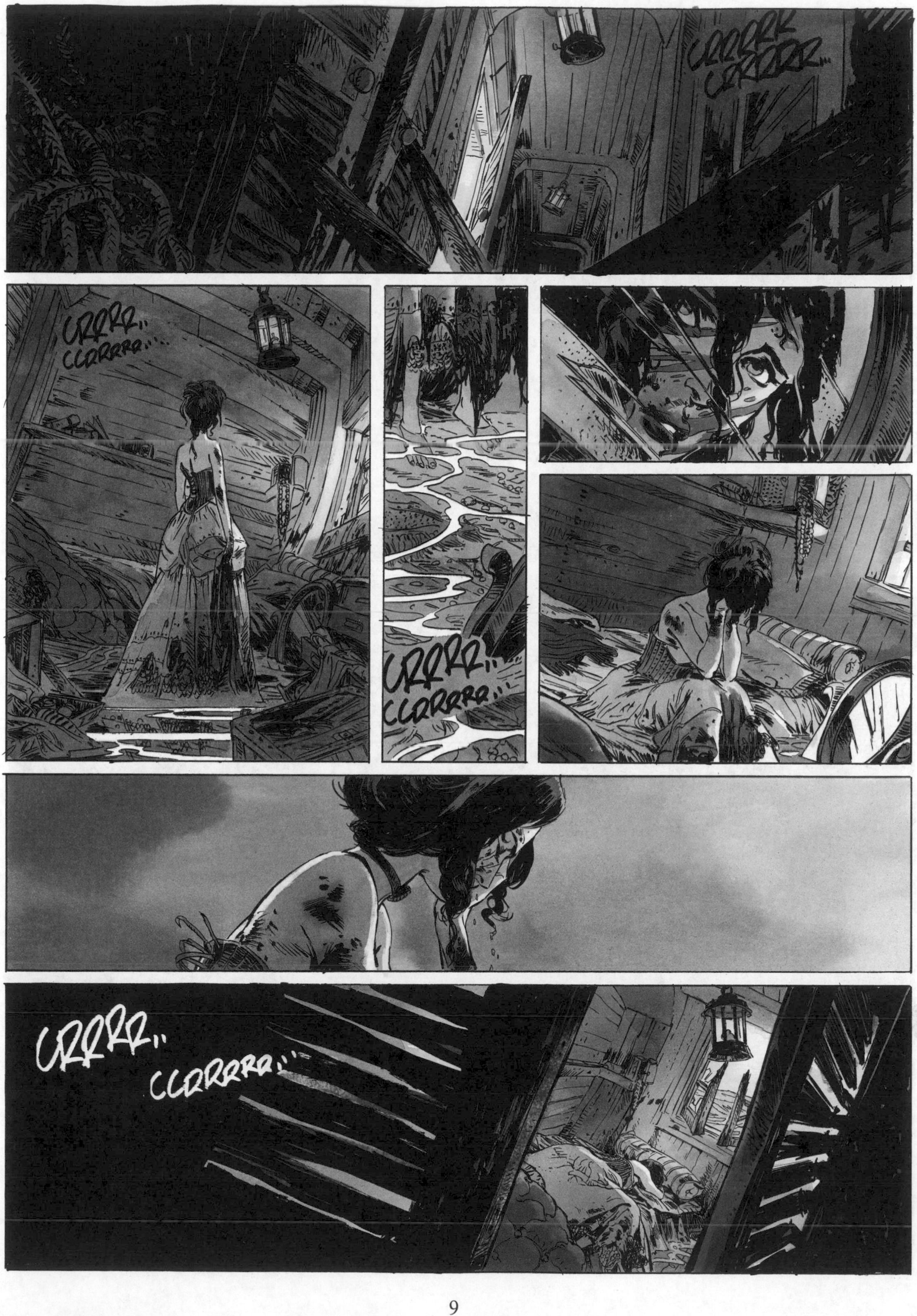
CRRRRK
CRRRRR...
CRRRR..
CLRRRRR...
CRRRR..
CLRRRRR...
CRRRR..
CLRRRRR...

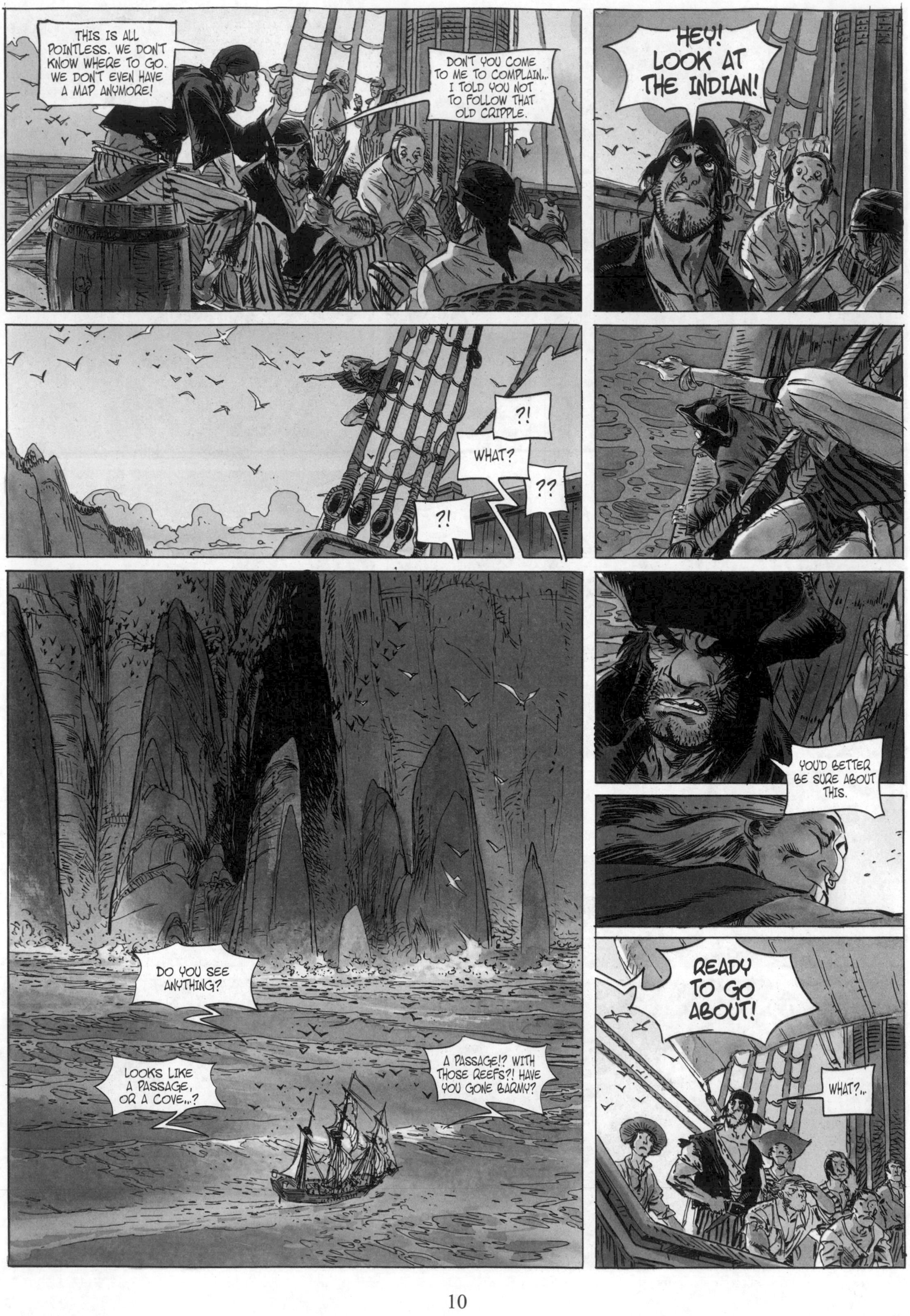
THIS IS ALL POINTLESS. WE DON'T KNOW WHERE TO GO. WE DON'T EVEN HAVE A MAP ANYMORE!
DON'T YOU COME TO ME TO COMPLAIN... I TOLD YOU NOT TO FOLLOW THAT OLD CRIPPLE.
HEY! LOOK AT THE INDIAN!
?!
WHAT?
??
?!
YOU'D BETTER BE SURE ABOUT THIS.
DO YOU SEE ANYTHING?
LOOKS LIKE A PASSAGE, OR A COVE...?
A PASSAGE!? WITH THOSE REEFS?! HAVE YOU GONE BARMY?
READY TO GO ABOUT!
WHAT?...

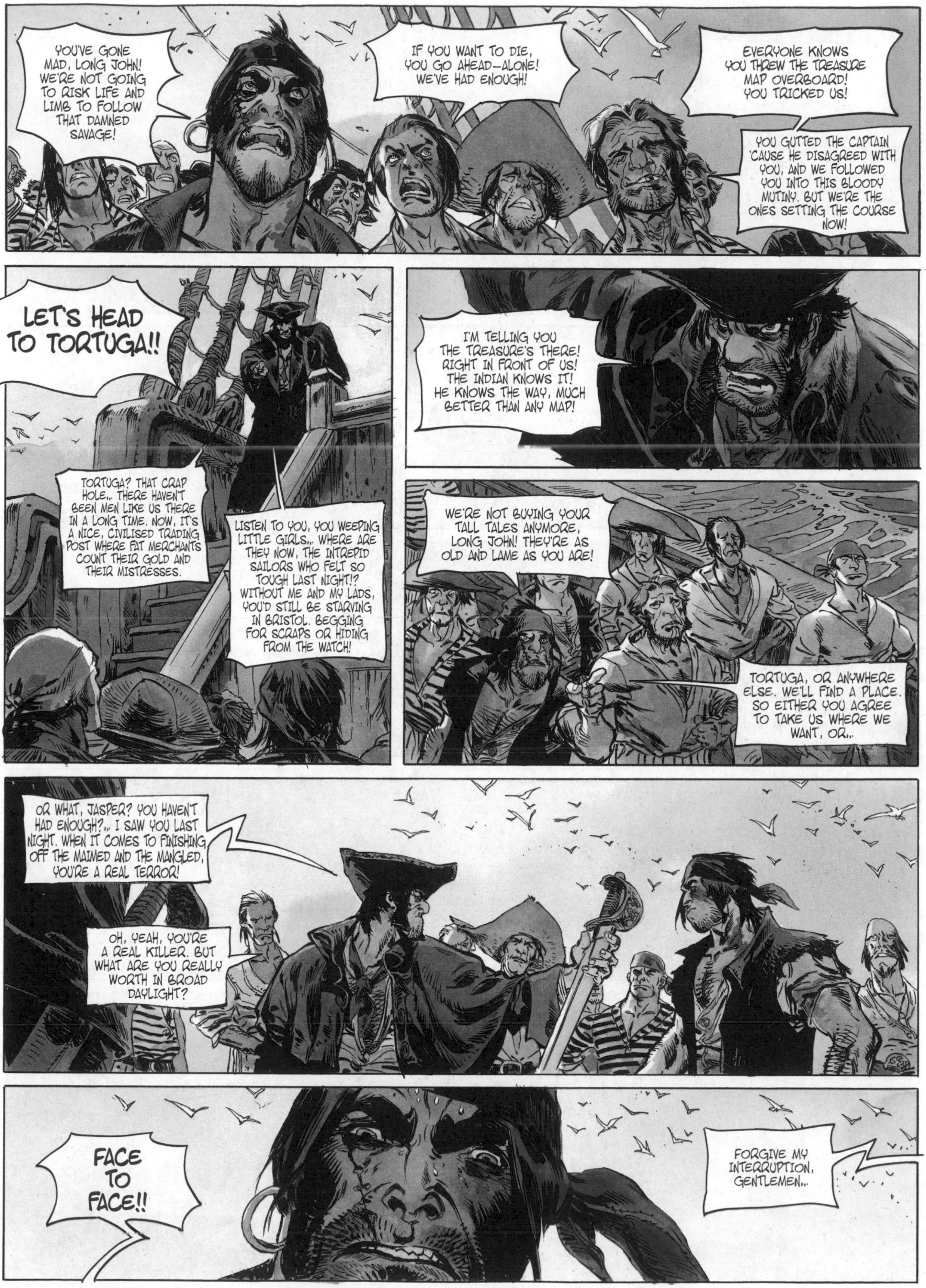

YOU'VE GONE MAD, LONG JOHN! WE'RE NOT GOING TO RISK LIFE AND LIMB TO FOLLOW THAT DAMNED SAVAGE!
IF YOU WANT TO DIE, YOU GO AHEAD–ALONE! WE'VE HAD ENOUGH!
EVERYONE KNOWS YOU THREW THE TREASURE MAP OVERBOARD! YOU TRICKED US!
YOU GUTTED THE CAPTAIN 'CAUSE HE DISAGREED WITH YOU, AND WE FOLLOWED YOU INTO THIS BLOODY MUTINY. BUT WE'RE THE ONES SETTING THE COURSE NOW!
LET'S HEAD TO TORTUGA!!
TORTUGA? THAT CRAP HOLE.. THERE HAVEN'T BEEN MEN LIKE US THERE IN A LONG TIME. NOW, IT'S A NICE, CIVILISED TRADING POST WHERE FAT MERCHANTS COUNT THEIR GOLD AND THEIR MISTRESSES.
LISTEN TO YOU, YOU WEEPING LITTLE GIRLS.. WHERE ARE THEY NOW, THE INTREPID SAILORS WHO FELT SO TOUGH LAST NIGHT!? WITHOUT ME AND MY LADS, YOU'D STILL BE STARVING IN BRISTOL. BEGGING FOR SCRAPS OR HIDING FROM THE WATCH!
I'M TELLING YOU THE TREASURE'S THERE! RIGHT IN FRONT OF US! THE INDIAN KNOWS IT! HE KNOWS THE WAY, MUCH BETTER THAN ANY MAP!
WE'RE NOT BUYING YOUR TALL TALES ANYMORE, LONG JOHN! THEY'RE AS OLD AND LAME AS YOU ARE!
TORTUGA, OR ANYWHERE ELSE. WE'LL FIND A PLACE. SO EITHER YOU AGREE TO TAKE US WHERE WE WANT, OR..
OR WHAT, JASPER? YOU HAVEN'T HAD ENOUGH?.. I SAW YOU LAST NIGHT. WHEN IT COMES TO FINISHING OFF THE MAIMED AND THE MANGLED, YOU'RE A REAL TERROR!
OH, YEAH, YOU'RE A REAL KILLER. BUT WHAT ARE YOU REALLY WORTH IN BROAD DAYLIGHT?
FACE TO FACE!!
FORGIVE MY INTERRUPTION, GENTLEMEN..

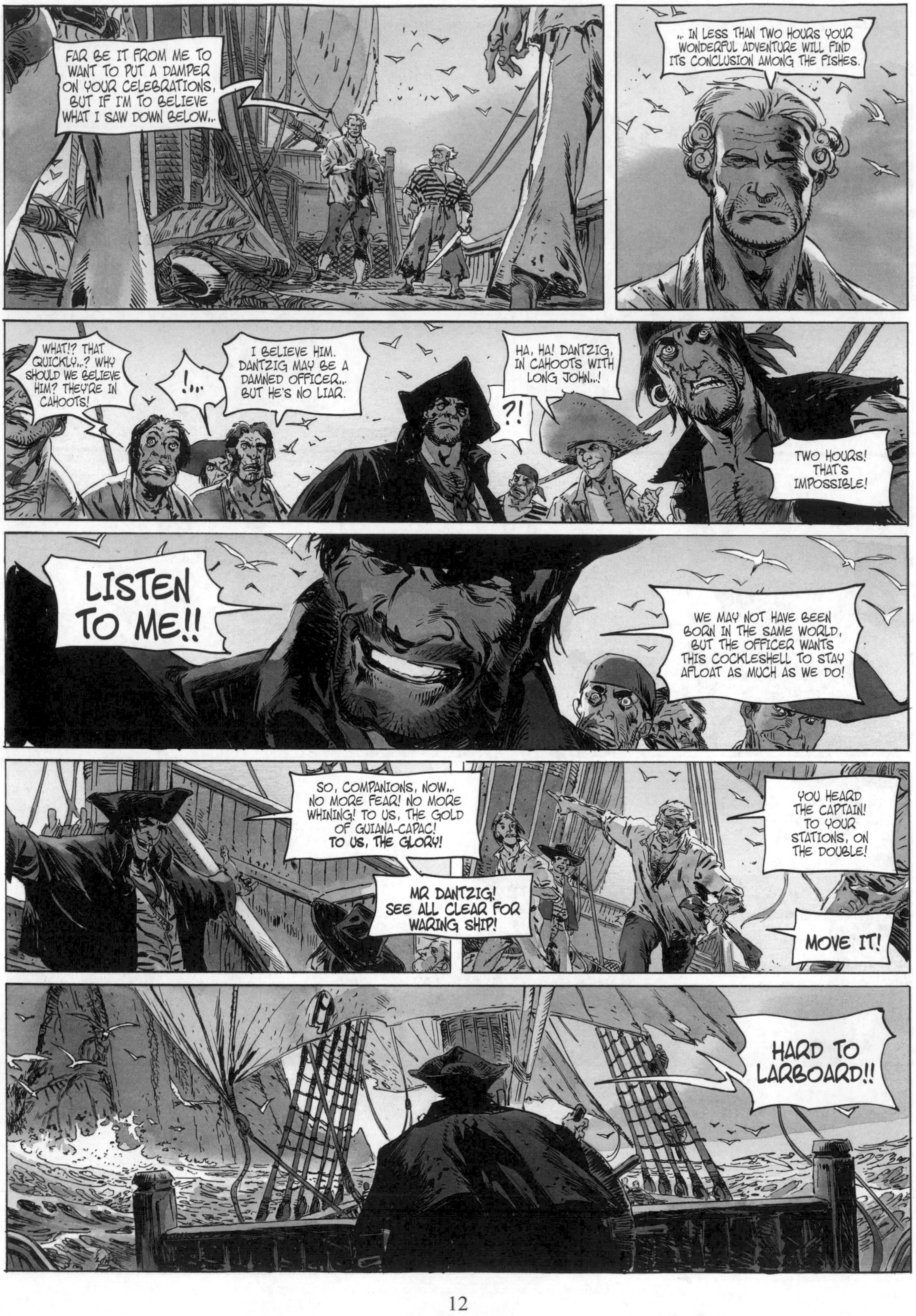

FAR BE IT FROM ME TO WANT TO PUT A DAMPER ON YOUR CELEBRATIONS, BUT IF I'M TO BELIEVE WHAT I SAW DOWN BELOW...
... IN LESS THAN TWO HOURS YOUR WONDERFUL ADVENTURE WILL FIND ITS CONCLUSION AMONG THE FISHES.
WHAT!? THAT QUICKLY...? WHY SHOULD WE BELIEVE HIM? THEY'RE IN CAHOOTS!
!...
I BELIEVE HIM. DANTZIG MAY BE A DAMNED OFFICER... BUT HE'S NO LIAR.
?!
HA, HA! DANTZIG, IN CAHOOTS WITH LONG JOHN...!
TWO HOURS! THAT'S IMPOSSIBLE!
LISTEN TO ME!!
WE MAY NOT HAVE BEEN BORN IN THE SAME WORLD, BUT THE OFFICER WANTS THIS COCKLESHELL TO STAY AFLOAT AS MUCH AS WE DO!
SO, COMPANIONS, NOW... NO MORE FEAR! NO MORE WHINING! TO US, THE GOLD OF GUIANA-CAPAC! TO US, THE GLORY!
MR DANTZIG! SEE ALL CLEAR FOR WARING SHIP!
YOU HEARD THE CAPTAIN! TO YOUR STATIONS, ON THE DOUBLE!
MOVE IT!
HARD TO LARBOARD!!

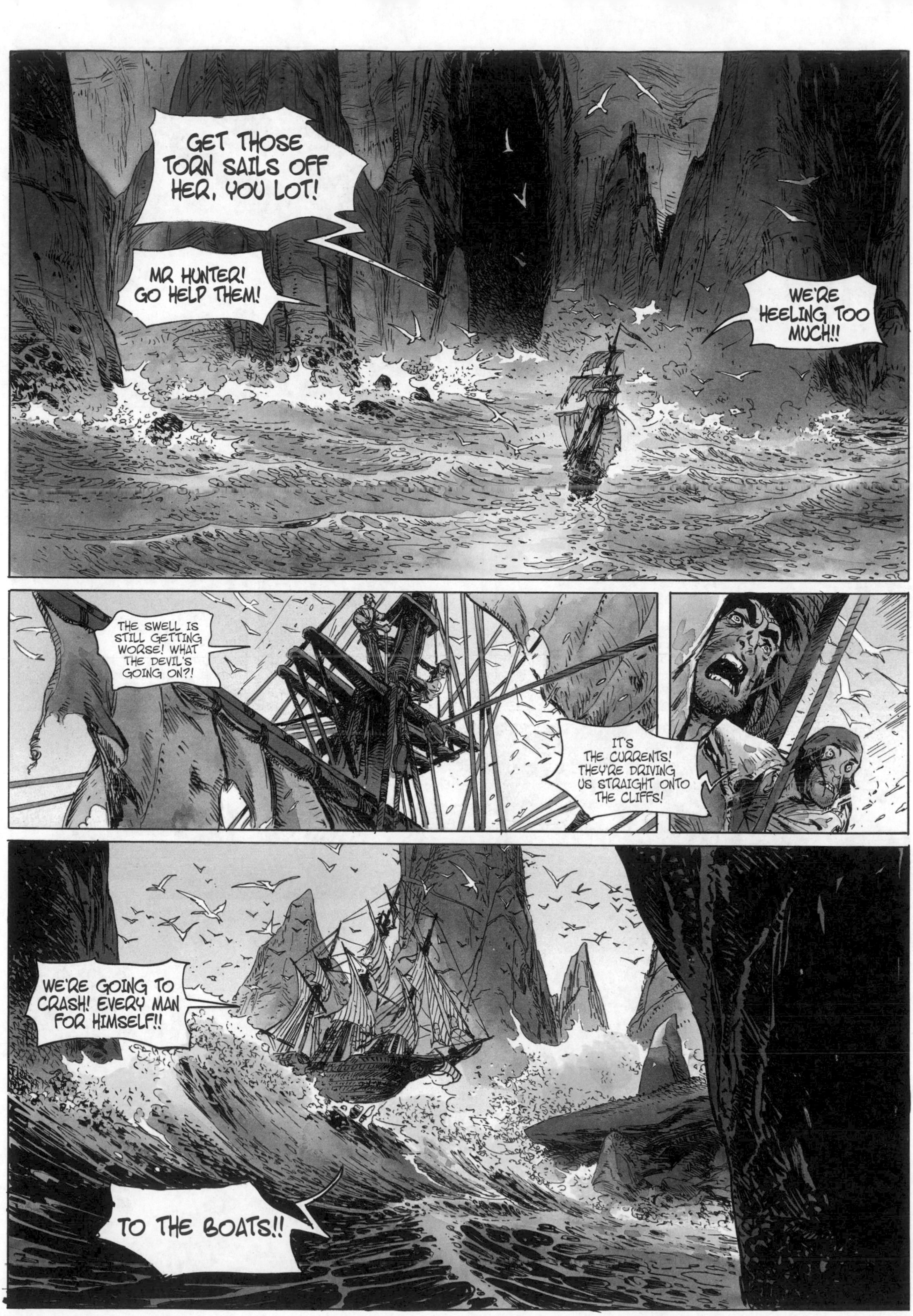
GET THOSE TORN SAILS OFF HER, YOU LOT!
MR HUNTER! GO HELP THEM!
WE'RE HEELING TOO MUCH!!
THE SWELL IS STILL GETTING WORSE! WHAT THE DEVIL'S GOING ON?!
IT'S THE CURRENTS! THEY'RE DRIVING US STRAIGHT ONTO THE CLIFFS!
WE'RE GOING TO CRASH! EVERY MAN FOR HIMSELF!!
TO THE BOATS!!

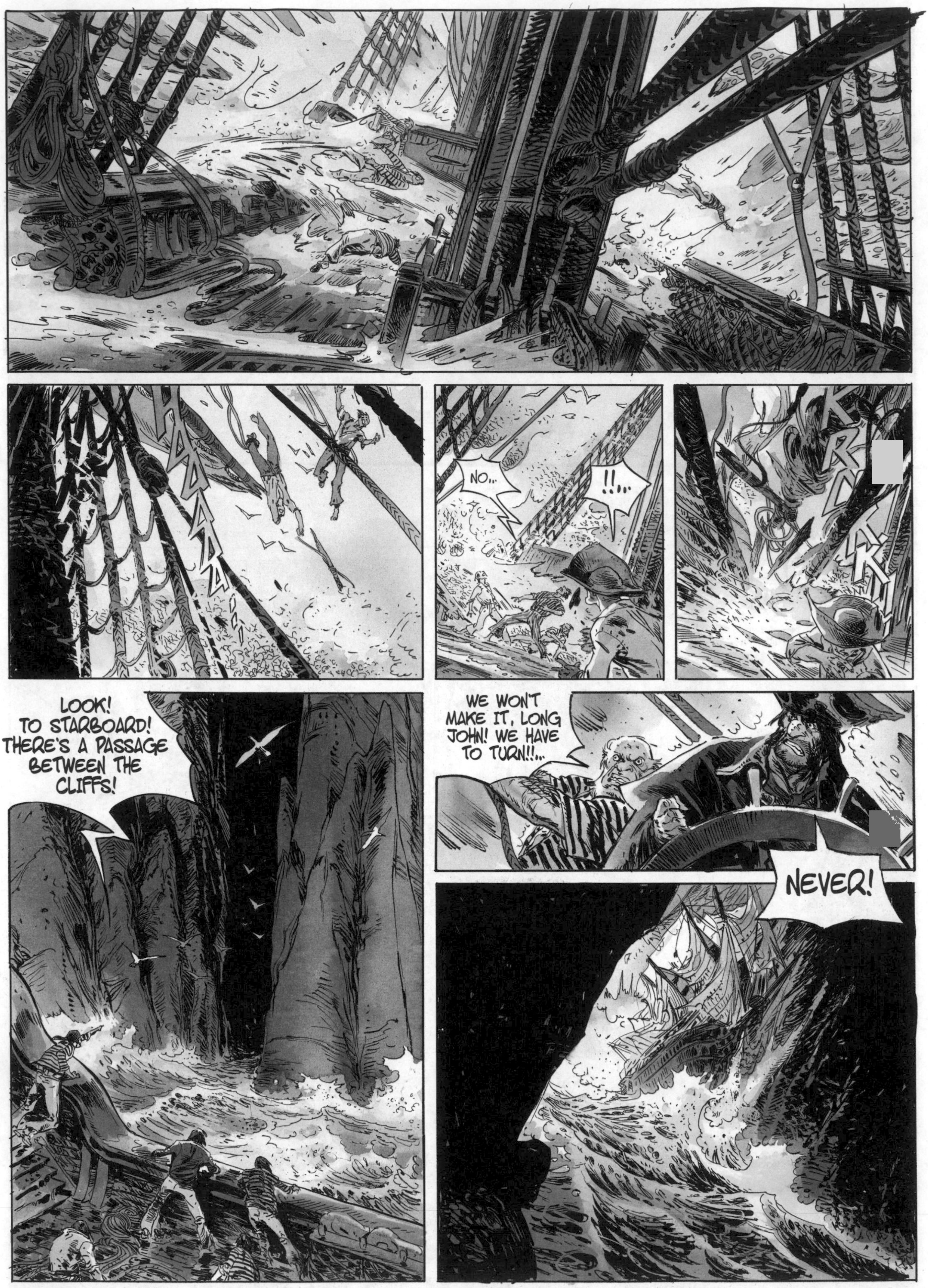
NO...
!!...
LOOK! TO STARBOARD! THERE'S A PASSAGE BETWEEN THE CLIFFS!
WE WON'T MAKE IT, LONG JOHN! WE HAVE TO TURN!!...
NEVER!

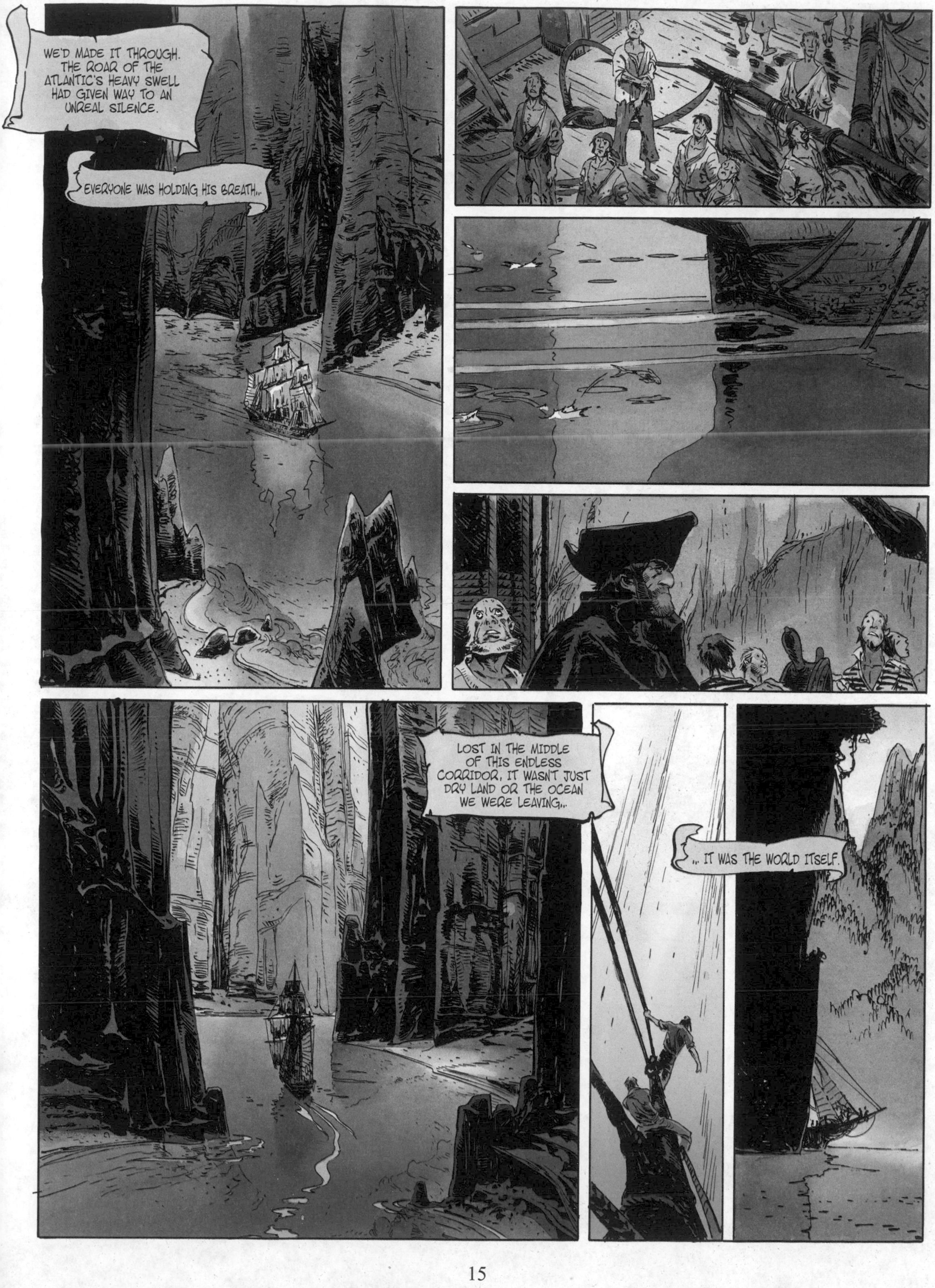
WE'D MADE IT THROUGH. THE ROAR OF THE ATLANTIC'S HEAVY SWELL HAD GIVEN WAY TO AN UNREAL SILENCE.
EVERYONE WAS HOLDING HIS BREATH...
LOST IN THE MIDDLE OF THIS ENDLESS CORRIDOR, IT WASN'T JUST DRY LAND OR THE OCEAN WE WERE LEAVING...
... IT WAS THE WORLD ITSELF.

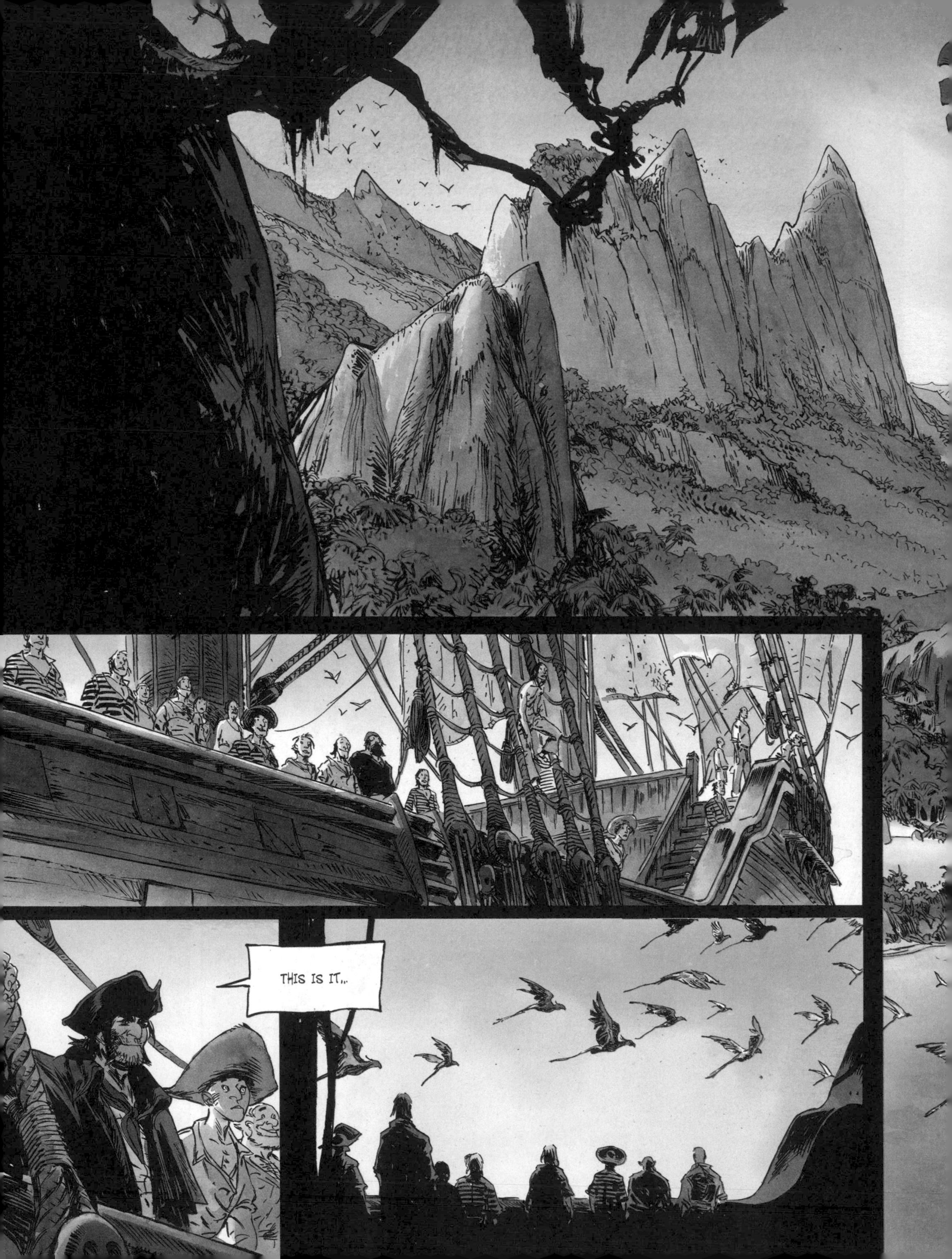
THIS IS IT...

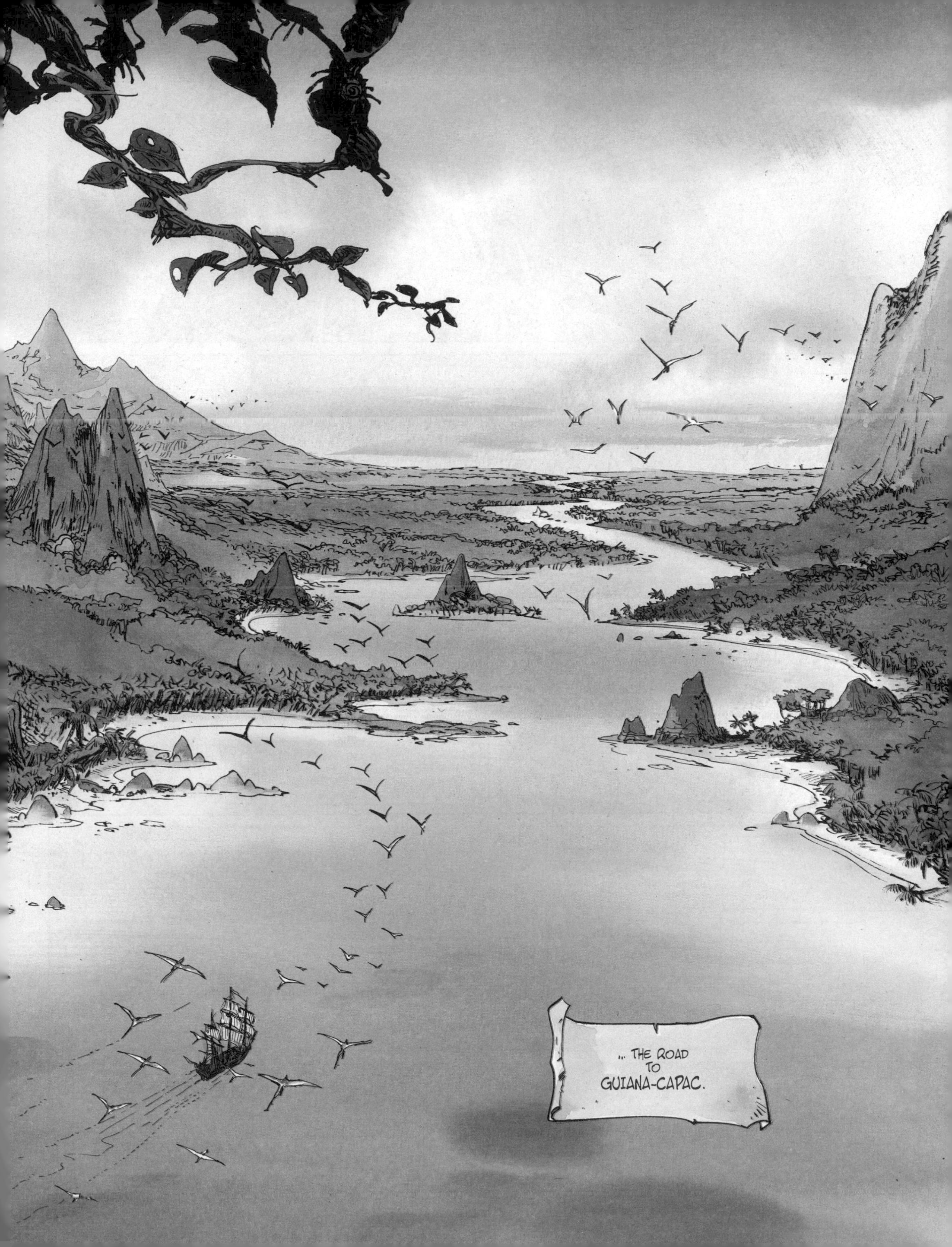
.. THE ROAD TO GUIANA-CAPAC.

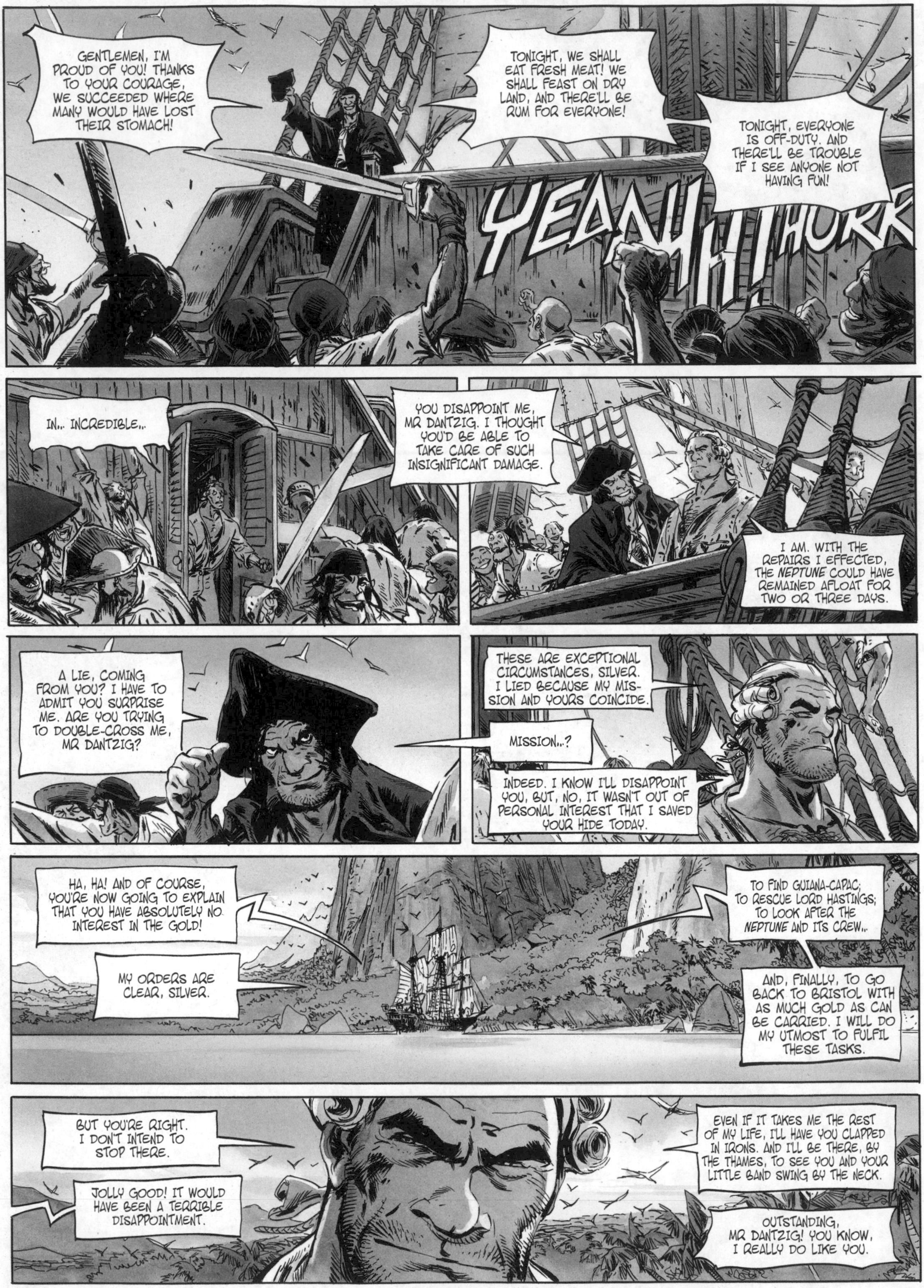
GENTLEMEN, I'M PROUD OF YOU! THANKS TO YOUR COURAGE, WE SUCCEEDED WHERE MANY WOULD HAVE LOST THEIR STOMACH!
TONIGHT, WE SHALL EAT FRESH MEAT! WE SHALL FEAST ON DRY LAND, AND THERE'LL BE RUM FOR EVERYONE!
TONIGHT, EVERYONE IS OFF-DUTY. AND THERE'LL BE TROUBLE IF I SEE ANYONE NOT HAVING FUN!
YEAAHH! HURR
IN... INCREDIBLE...
YOU DISAPPOINT ME, MR DANTZIG. I THOUGHT YOU'D BE ABLE TO TAKE CARE OF SUCH INSIGNIFICANT DAMAGE.
I AM. WITH THE REPAIRS I EFFECTED, THE NEPTUNE COULD HAVE REMAINED AFLOAT FOR TWO OR THREE DAYS.
A LIE, COMING FROM YOU? I HAVE TO ADMIT YOU SURPRISE ME. ARE YOU TRYING TO DOUBLE-CROSS ME, MR DANTZIG?
THESE ARE EXCEPTIONAL CIRCUMSTANCES, SILVER. I LIED BECAUSE MY MISSION AND YOURS COINCIDE.
MISSION...?
INDEED. I KNOW I'LL DISAPPOINT YOU, BUT, NO, IT WASN'T OUT OF PERSONAL INTEREST THAT I SAVED YOUR HIDE TODAY.
HA, HA! AND OF COURSE, YOU'RE NOW GOING TO EXPLAIN THAT YOU HAVE ABSOLUTELY NO INTEREST IN THE GOLD!
MY ORDERS ARE CLEAR, SILVER.
TO FIND GUIANA-CAPAC; TO RESCUE LORD HASTINGS; TO LOOK AFTER THE NEPTUNE AND ITS CREW...
AND, FINALLY, TO GO BACK TO BRISTOL WITH AS MUCH GOLD AS CAN BE CARRIED. I WILL DO MY UTMOST TO FULFIL THESE TASKS.
BUT YOU'RE RIGHT. I DON'T INTEND TO STOP THERE.
JOLLY GOOD! IT WOULD HAVE BEEN A TERRIBLE DISAPPOINTMENT.
EVEN IF IT TAKES ME THE REST OF MY LIFE, I'LL HAVE YOU CLAPPED IN IRONS. AND I'LL BE THERE, BY THE THAMES, TO SEE YOU AND YOUR LITTLE BAND SWING BY THE NECK.
OUTSTANDING, MR DANTZIG! YOU KNOW, I REALLY DO LIKE YOU.

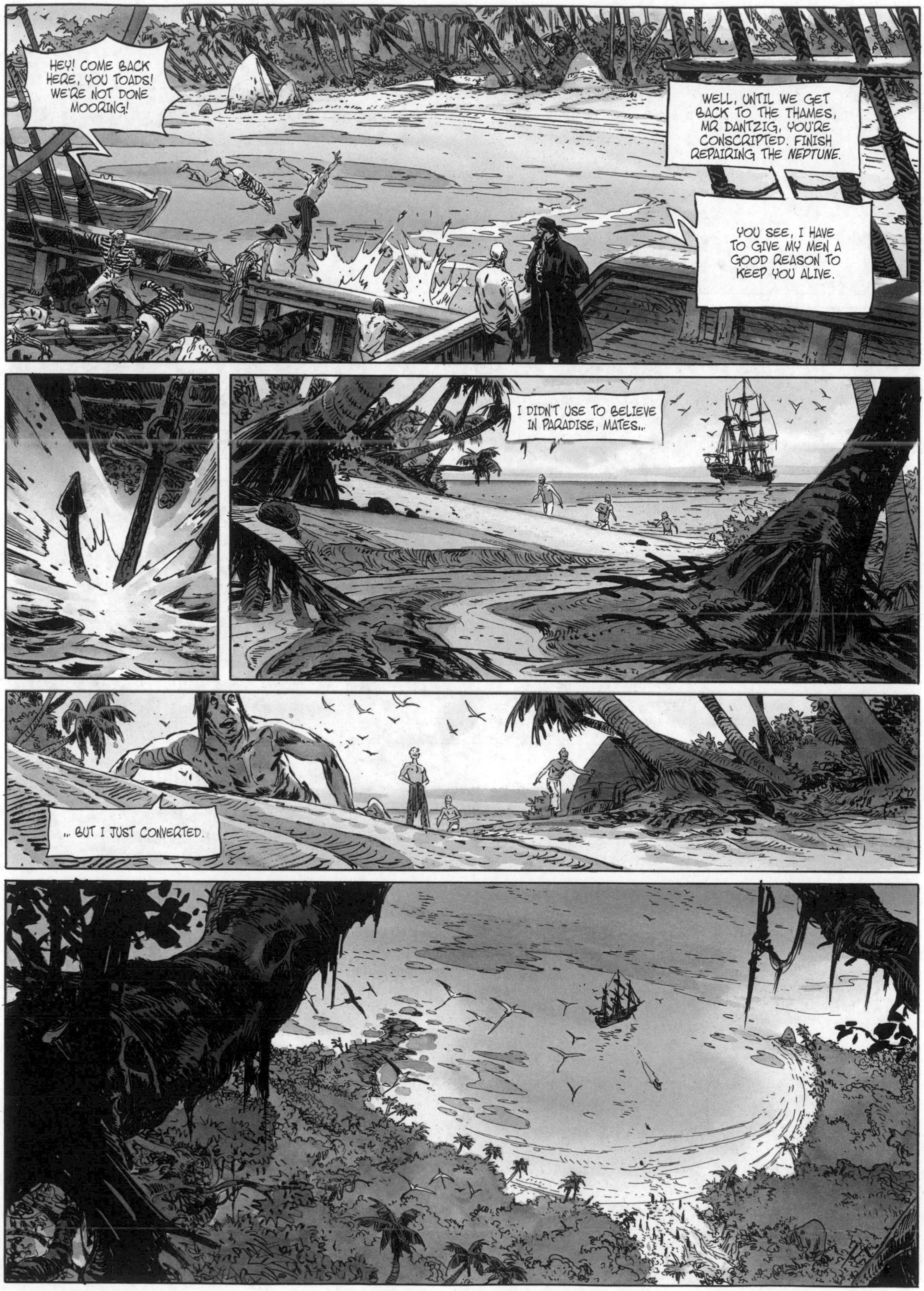
HEY! COME BACK HERE, YOU TOADS! WE'RE NOT DONE MOORING!
WELL, UNTIL WE GET BACK TO THE THAMES, MR DANTZIG, YOU'RE CONSCRIPTED. FINISH REPAIRING THE *NEPTUNE*.
YOU SEE, I HAVE TO GIVE MY MEN A GOOD REASON TO KEEP YOU ALIVE.
I DIDN'T USE TO BELIEVE IN PARADISE, MATES...
... BUT I JUST CONVERTED.

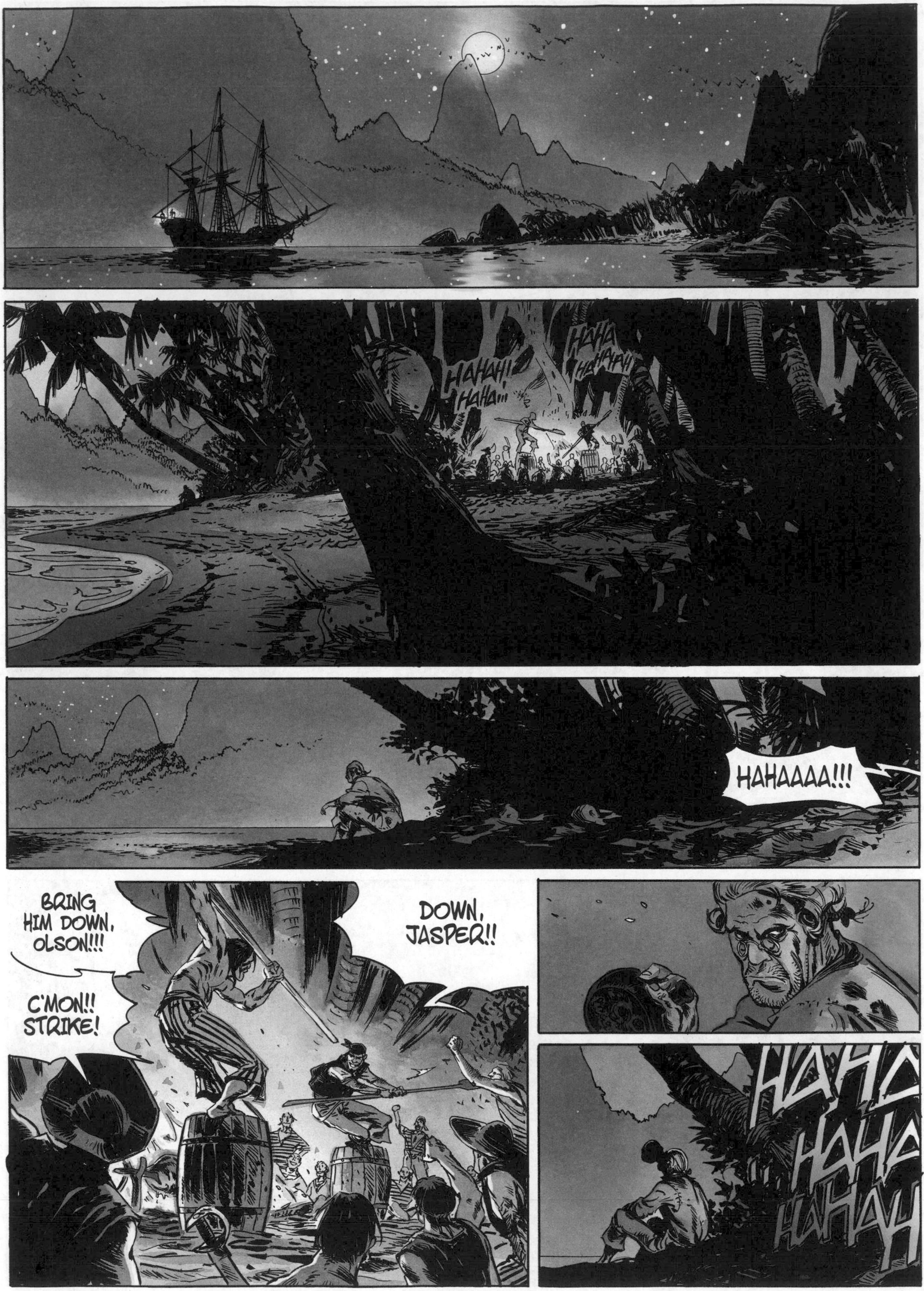
HAHAH!
HAHA...
HAHAAAA!!!
BRING HIM DOWN, OLSON!!!
C'MON!! STRIKE!
DOWN, JASPER!!

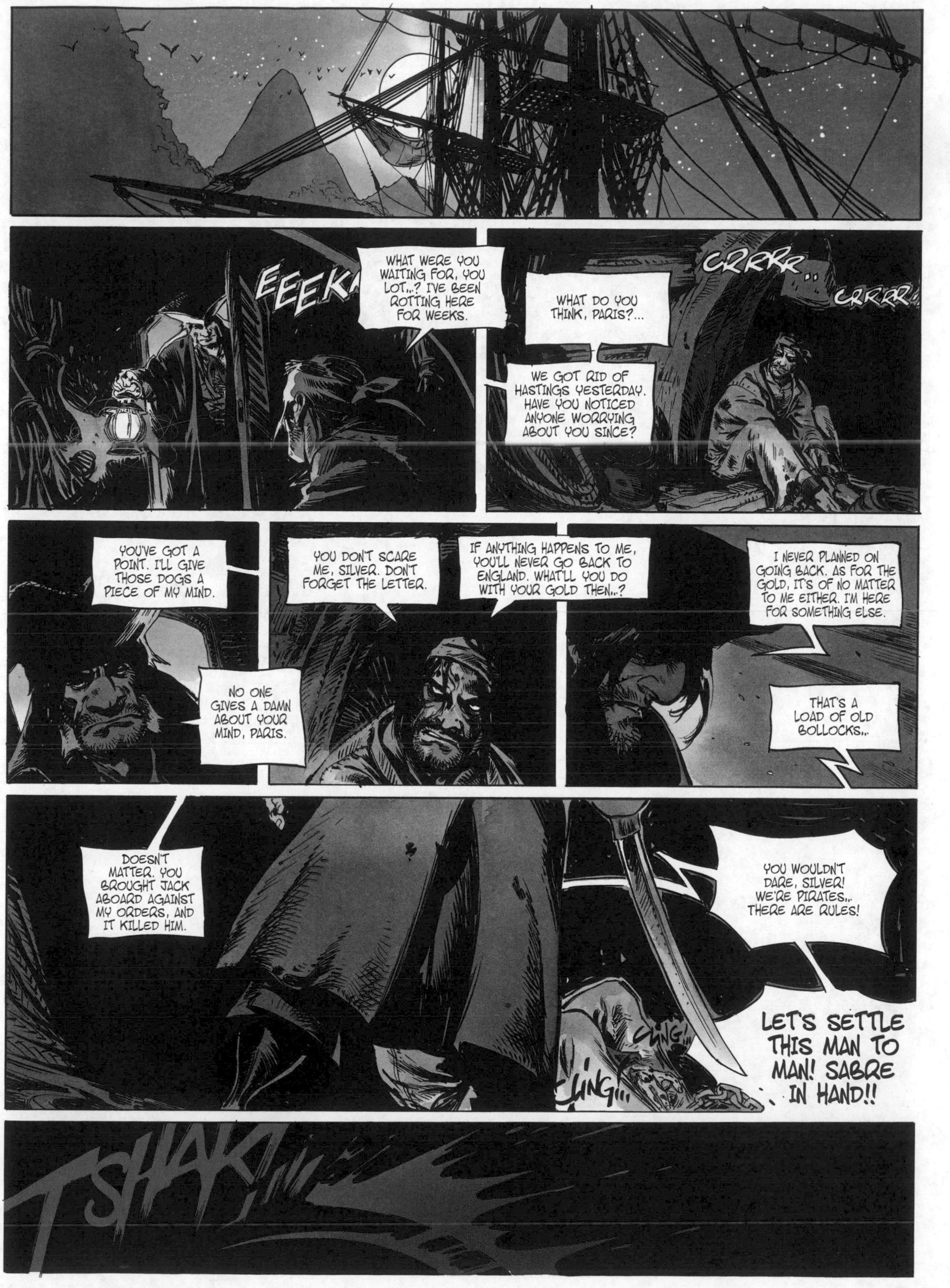
EEEKA
WHAT WERE YOU WAITING FOR, YOU LOT...? I'VE BEEN ROTTING HERE FOR WEEKS.
CRRRR.. CRRRR..
WHAT DO YOU THINK, PARIS?...
WE GOT RID OF HASTINGS YESTERDAY. HAVE YOU NOTICED ANYONE WORRYING ABOUT YOU SINCE?
YOU'VE GOT A POINT. I'LL GIVE THOSE DOGS A PIECE OF MY MIND.
NO ONE GIVES A DAMN ABOUT YOUR MIND, PARIS.
YOU DON'T SCARE ME, SILVER. DON'T FORGET THE LETTER.
IF ANYTHING HAPPENS TO ME, YOU'LL NEVER GO BACK TO ENGLAND. WHAT'LL YOU DO WITH YOUR GOLD THEN...?
I NEVER PLANNED ON GOING BACK. AS FOR THE GOLD, IT'S OF NO MATTER TO ME EITHER. I'M HERE FOR SOMETHING ELSE.
THAT'S A LOAD OF OLD BOLLOCKS...
DOESN'T MATTER. YOU BROUGHT JACK ABOARD AGAINST MY ORDERS, AND IT KILLED HIM.
YOU WOULDN'T DARE, SILVER! WE'RE PIRATES... THERE ARE RULES!
LET'S SETTLE THIS MAN TO MAN! SABRE IN HAND!!
CLING!..
CLING!..
TSHAK!!!

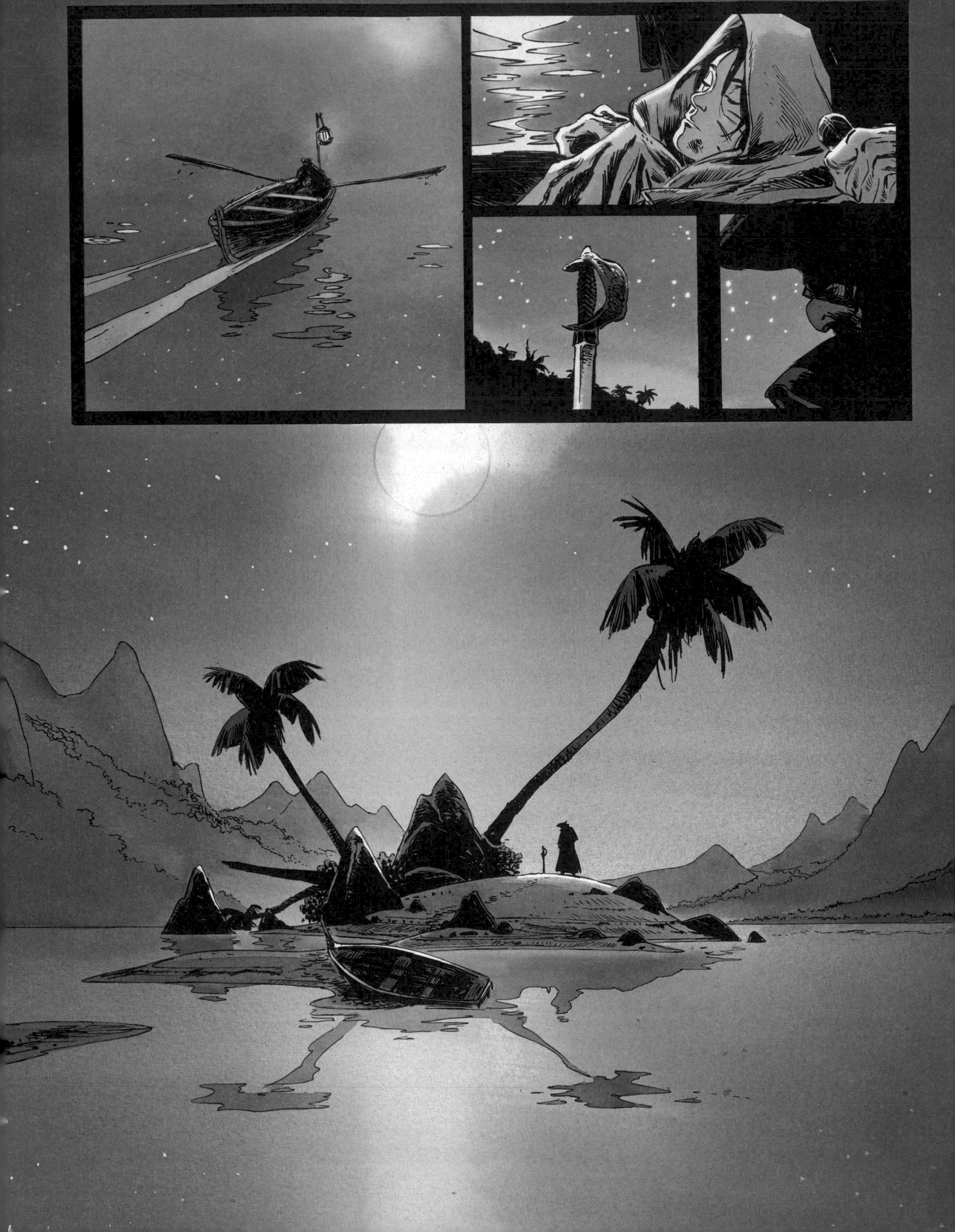

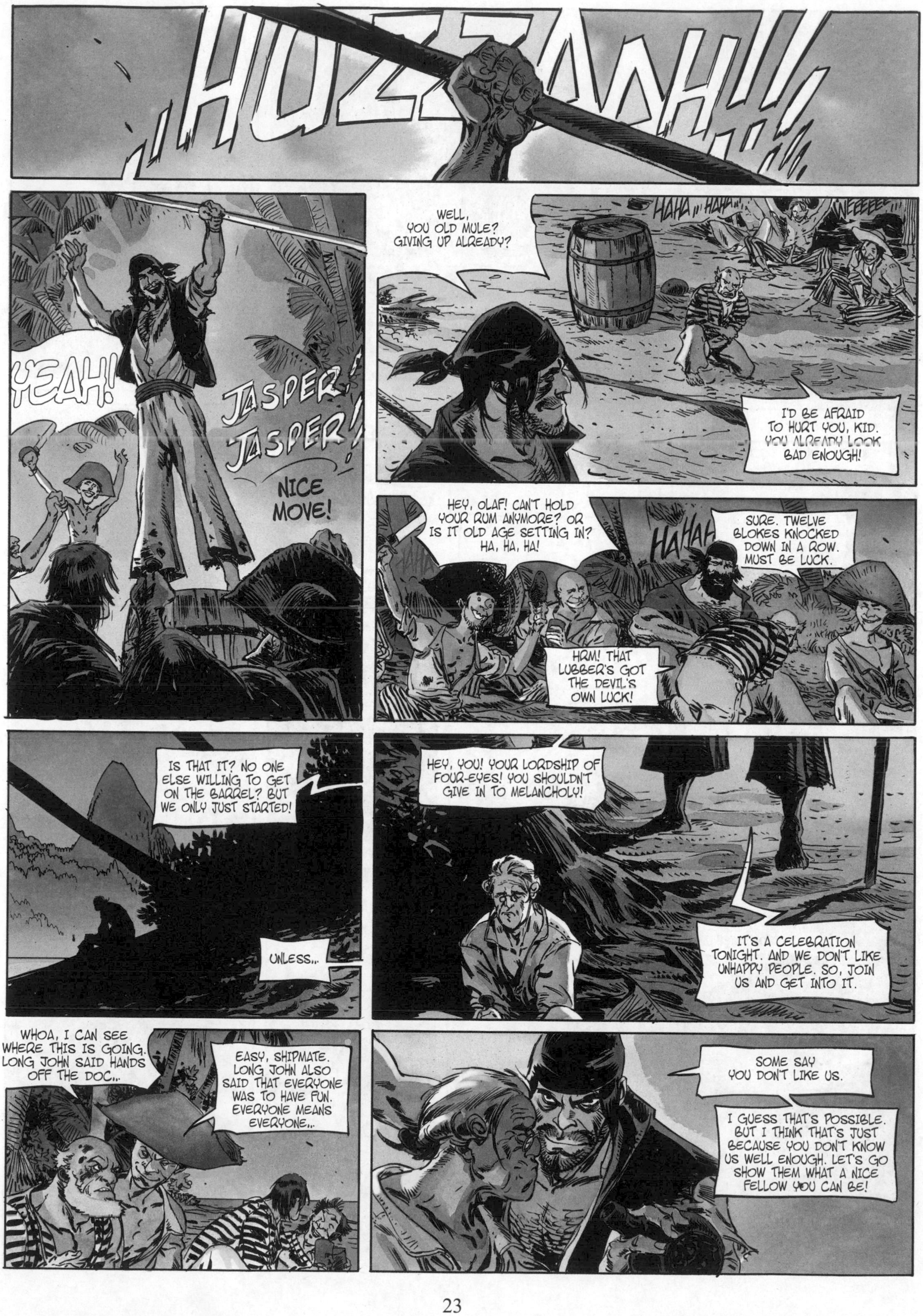
HUZZAAH!!
YEAH!
JASPER! JASPER!
NICE MOVE!
WELL, YOU OLD MULE? GIVING UP ALREADY?
HAHA HAHA
WEEEEE
I'D BE AFRAID TO HURT YOU, KID. YOU ALREADY LOOK BAD ENOUGH!
HEY, OLAF! CAN'T HOLD YOUR RUM ANYMORE? OR IS IT OLD AGE SETTING IN? HA, HA, HA!
HAHAH
SURE. TWELVE BLOKES KNOCKED DOWN IN A ROW. MUST BE LUCK.
HRM! THAT LUBBER'S GOT THE DEVIL'S OWN LUCK!
IS THAT IT? NO ONE ELSE WILLING TO GET ON THE BARREL? BUT WE ONLY JUST STARTED!
UNLESS...
HEY, YOU! YOUR LORDSHIP OF FOUR-EYES! YOU SHOULDN'T GIVE IN TO MELANCHOLY!
IT'S A CELEBRATION TONIGHT. AND WE DON'T LIKE UNHAPPY PEOPLE. SO, JOIN US AND GET INTO IT.
WHOA, I CAN SEE WHERE THIS IS GOING. LONG JOHN SAID HANDS OFF THE DOC...
EASY, SHIPMATE. LONG JOHN ALSO SAID THAT EVERYONE WAS TO HAVE FUN. EVERYONE MEANS EVERYONE...
SOME SAY YOU DON'T LIKE US.
I GUESS THAT'S POSSIBLE. BUT I THINK THAT'S JUST BECAUSE YOU DON'T KNOW US WELL ENOUGH. LET'S GO SHOW THEM WHAT A NICE FELLOW YOU CAN BE!

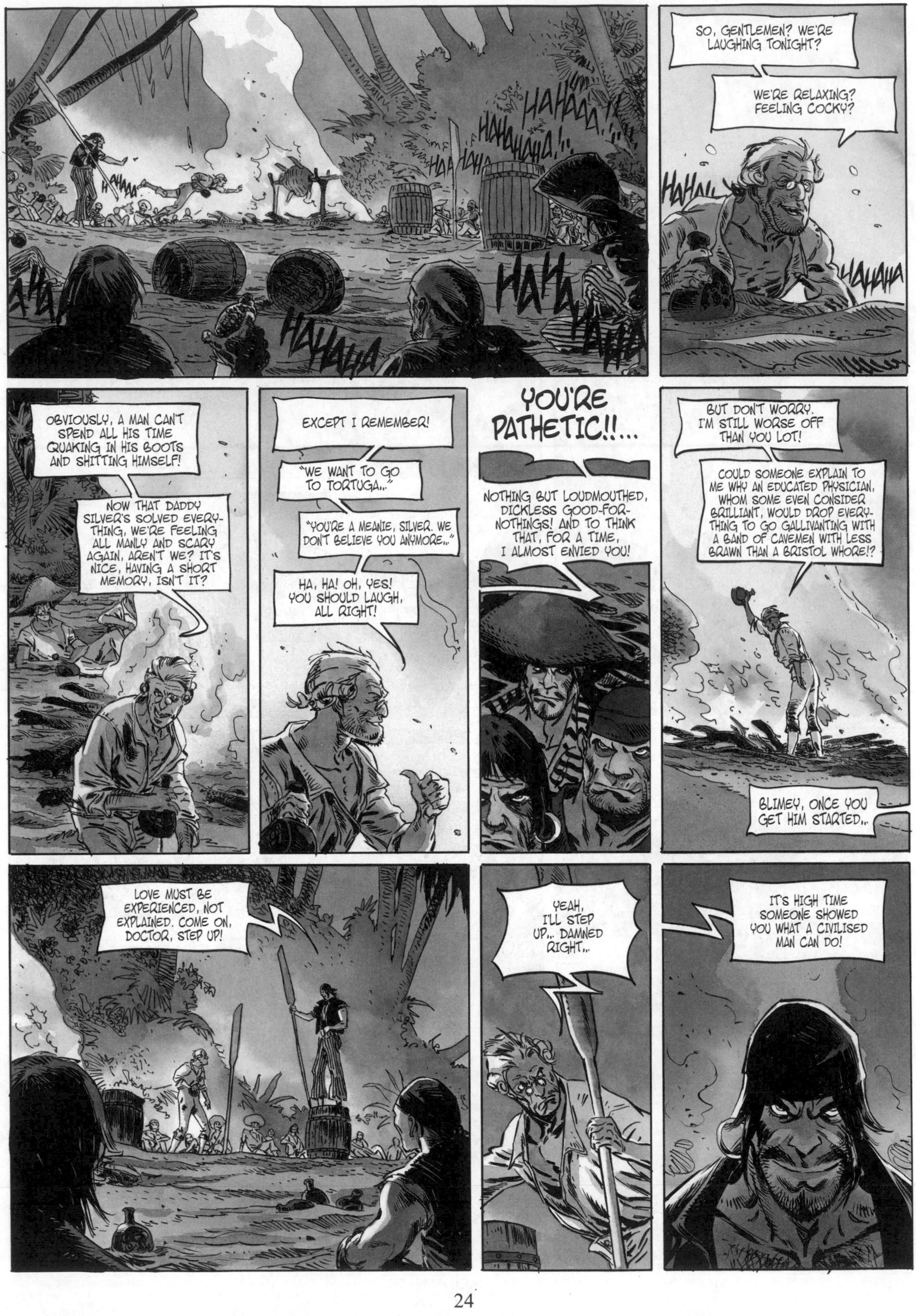
HAHAAA
HAHAHAHAHA!!..
HAAHAHA
HAHAAA
HAHAHA
HAHAHA
HAHAHAHA
SO, GENTLEMEN? WE'RE LAUGHING TONIGHT?
WE'RE RELAXING? FEELING COCKY?
HAHAH
HAHAHA
OBVIOUSLY, A MAN CAN'T SPEND ALL HIS TIME QUAKING IN HIS BOOTS AND SHITTING HIMSELF!
NOW THAT DADDY SILVER'S SOLVED EVERYTHING, WE'RE FEELING ALL MANLY AND SCARY AGAIN, AREN'T WE? IT'S NICE, HAVING A SHORT MEMORY, ISN'T IT?
EXCEPT I REMEMBER!
"WE WANT TO GO TO TORTUGA.."
"YOU'RE A MEANIE, SILVER. WE DON'T BELIEVE YOU ANYMORE.."
HA, HA! OH, YES! YOU SHOULD LAUGH, ALL RIGHT!
YOU'RE PATHETIC!!...
NOTHING BUT LOUDMOUTHED, DICKLESS GOOD-FOR-NOTHINGS! AND TO THINK THAT, FOR A TIME, I ALMOST ENVIED YOU!
BUT DON'T WORRY. I'M STILL WORSE OFF THAN YOU LOT!
COULD SOMEONE EXPLAIN TO ME WHY AN EDUCATED PHYSICIAN, WHOM SOME EVEN CONSIDER BRILLIANT, WOULD DROP EVERYTHING TO GO GALLIVANTING WITH A BAND OF CAVEMEN WITH LESS BRAWN THAN A BRISTOL WHORE!?
BLIMEY, ONCE YOU GET HIM STARTED..
LOVE MUST BE EXPERIENCED, NOT EXPLAINED. COME ON, DOCTOR, STEP UP!
YEAH, I'LL STEP UP.. DAMNED RIGHT..
IT'S HIGH TIME SOMEONE SHOWED YOU WHAT A CIVILISED MAN CAN DO!

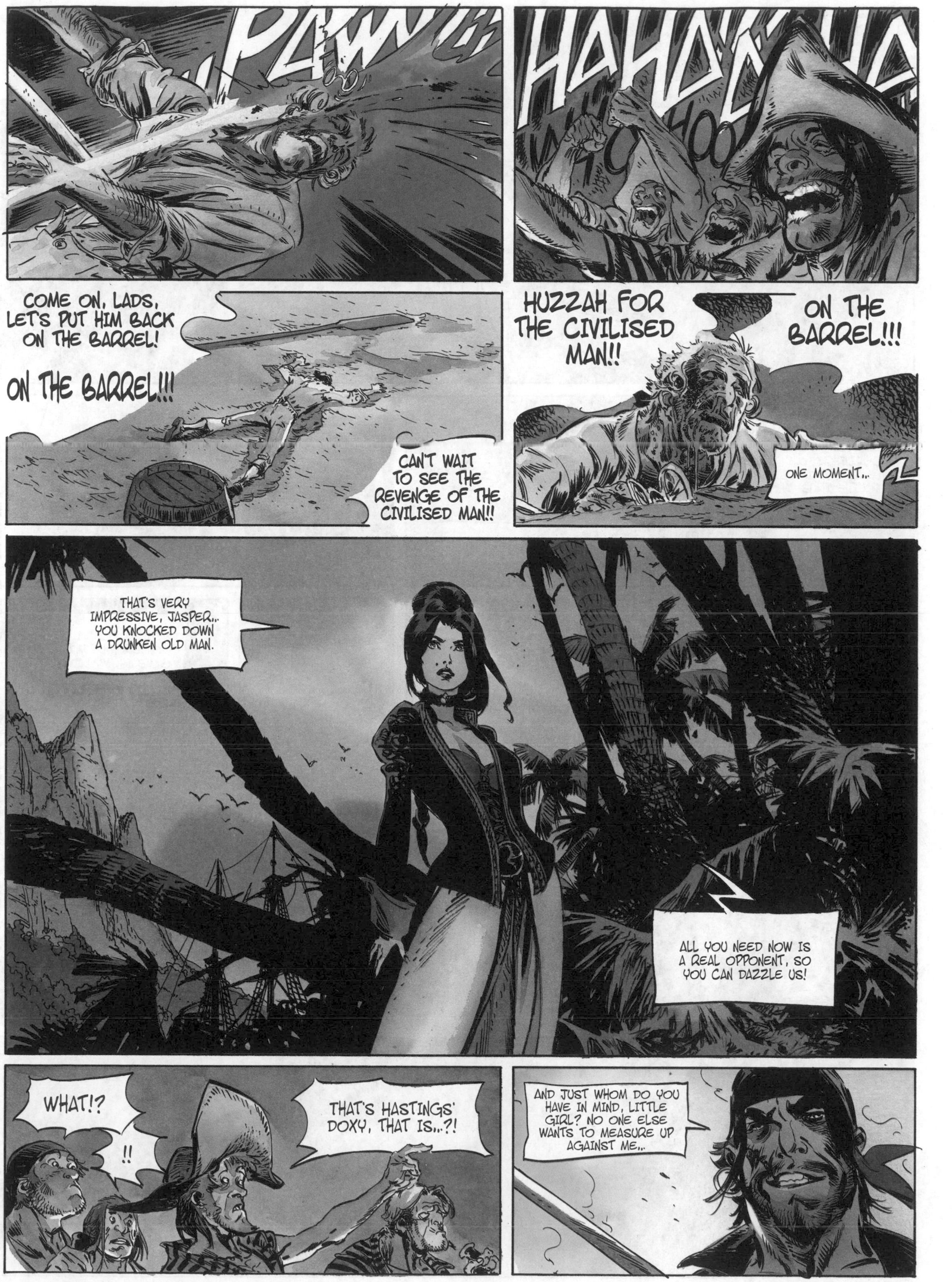
PAWN
HAHA
HAHA
HOO
HOO
COME ON, LADS, LET'S PUT HIM BACK ON THE BARREL!
ON THE BARREL!!!
CAN'T WAIT TO SEE THE REVENGE OF THE CIVILISED MAN!!
HUZZAH FOR THE CIVILISED MAN!!
ON THE BARREL!!!
ONE MOMENT...
THAT'S VERY IMPRESSIVE, JASPER... YOU KNOCKED DOWN A DRUNKEN OLD MAN.
ALL YOU NEED NOW IS A REAL OPPONENT, SO YOU CAN DAZZLE US!
WHAT!?
!!
THAT'S HASTINGS' DOXY, THAT IS...?!
AND JUST WHOM DO YOU HAVE IN MIND, LITTLE GIRL? NO ONE ELSE WANTS TO MEASURE UP AGAINST ME...

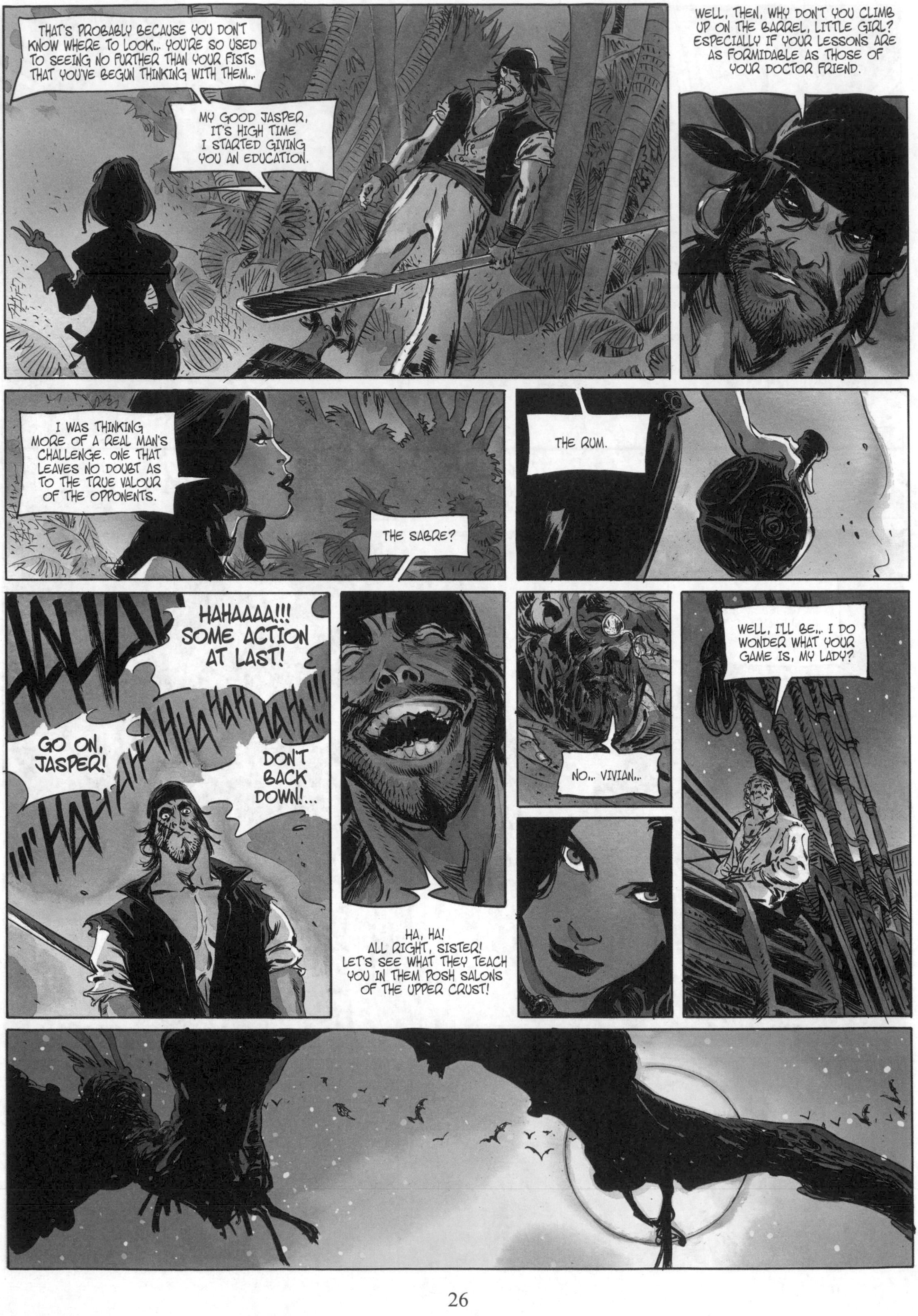
THAT'S PROBABLY BECAUSE YOU DON'T KNOW WHERE TO LOOK... YOU'RE SO USED TO SEEING NO FURTHER THAN YOUR FISTS THAT YOU'VE BEGUN THINKING WITH THEM...
MY GOOD JASPER, IT'S HIGH TIME I STARTED GIVING YOU AN EDUCATION.
WELL, THEN, WHY DON'T YOU CLIMB UP ON THE BARREL, LITTLE GIRL? ESPECIALLY IF YOUR LESSONS ARE AS FORMIDABLE AS THOSE OF YOUR DOCTOR FRIEND.
I WAS THINKING MORE OF A REAL MAN'S CHALLENGE. ONE THAT LEAVES NO DOUBT AS TO THE TRUE VALOUR OF THE OPPONENTS.
THE SABRE?
THE RUM.
HAHAAAA!!! SOME ACTION AT LAST!
GO ON, JASPER!
DON'T BACK DOWN!...
HA, HA! ALL RIGHT, SISTER! LET'S SEE WHAT THEY TEACH YOU IN THEM POSH SALONS OF THE UPPER CRUST!
NO... VIVIAN...
WELL, I'LL BE... I DO WONDER WHAT YOUR GAME IS, MY LADY?

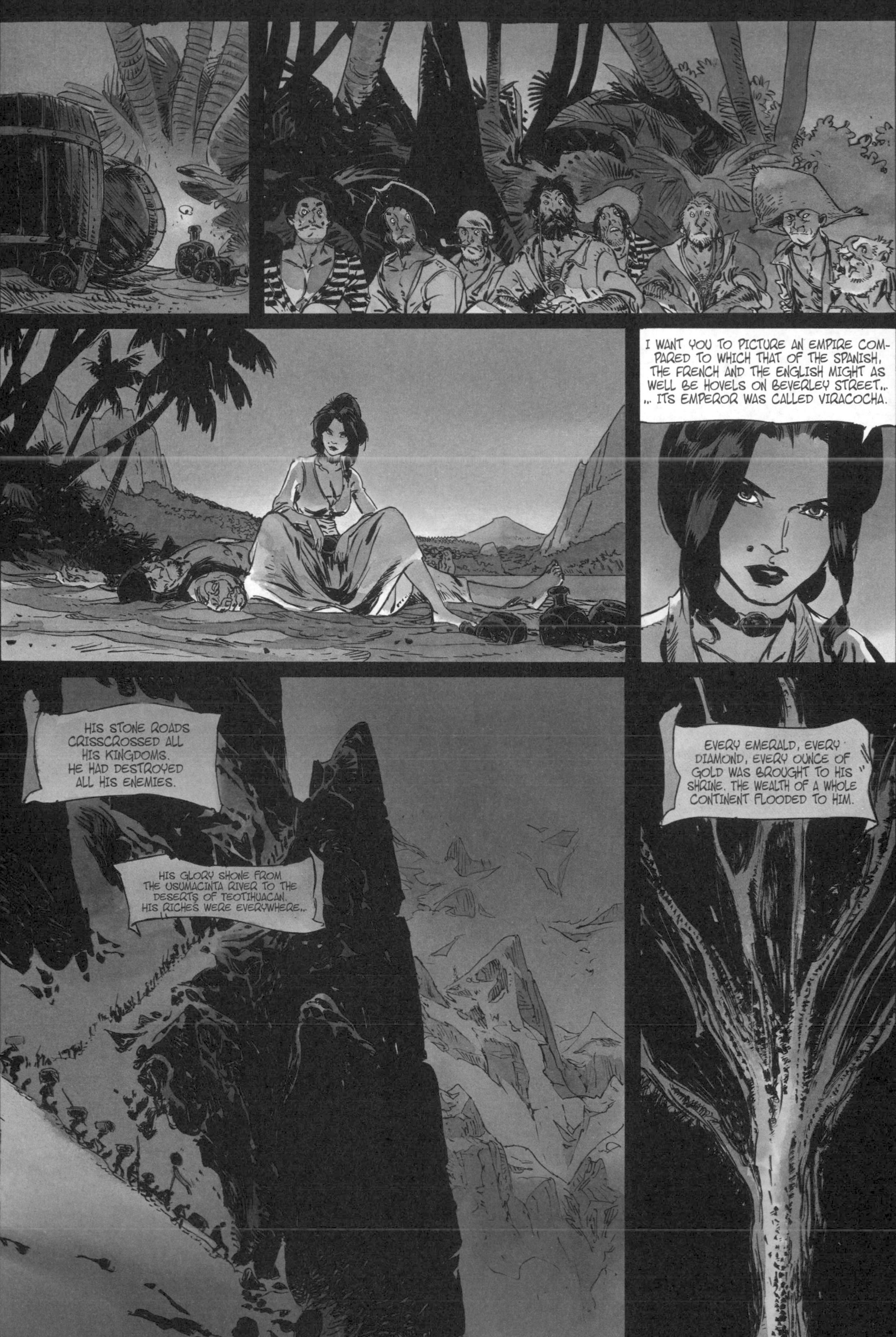
I WANT YOU TO PICTURE AN EMPIRE COMPARED TO WHICH THAT OF THE SPANISH, THE FRENCH AND THE ENGLISH MIGHT AS WELL BE HOVELS ON BEVERLEY STREET... ... ITS EMPEROR WAS CALLED VIRACOCHA.
HIS STONE ROADS CRISSCROSSED ALL HIS KINGDOMS. HE HAD DESTROYED ALL HIS ENEMIES.
HIS GLORY SHONE FROM THE USUMACINTA RIVER TO THE DESERTS OF TEOTIHUACAN. HIS RICHES WERE EVERYWHERE...
EVERY EMERALD, EVERY DIAMOND, EVERY OUNCE OF GOLD WAS BROUGHT TO HIS SHRINE. THE WEALTH OF A WHOLE CONTINENT FLOODED TO HIM.

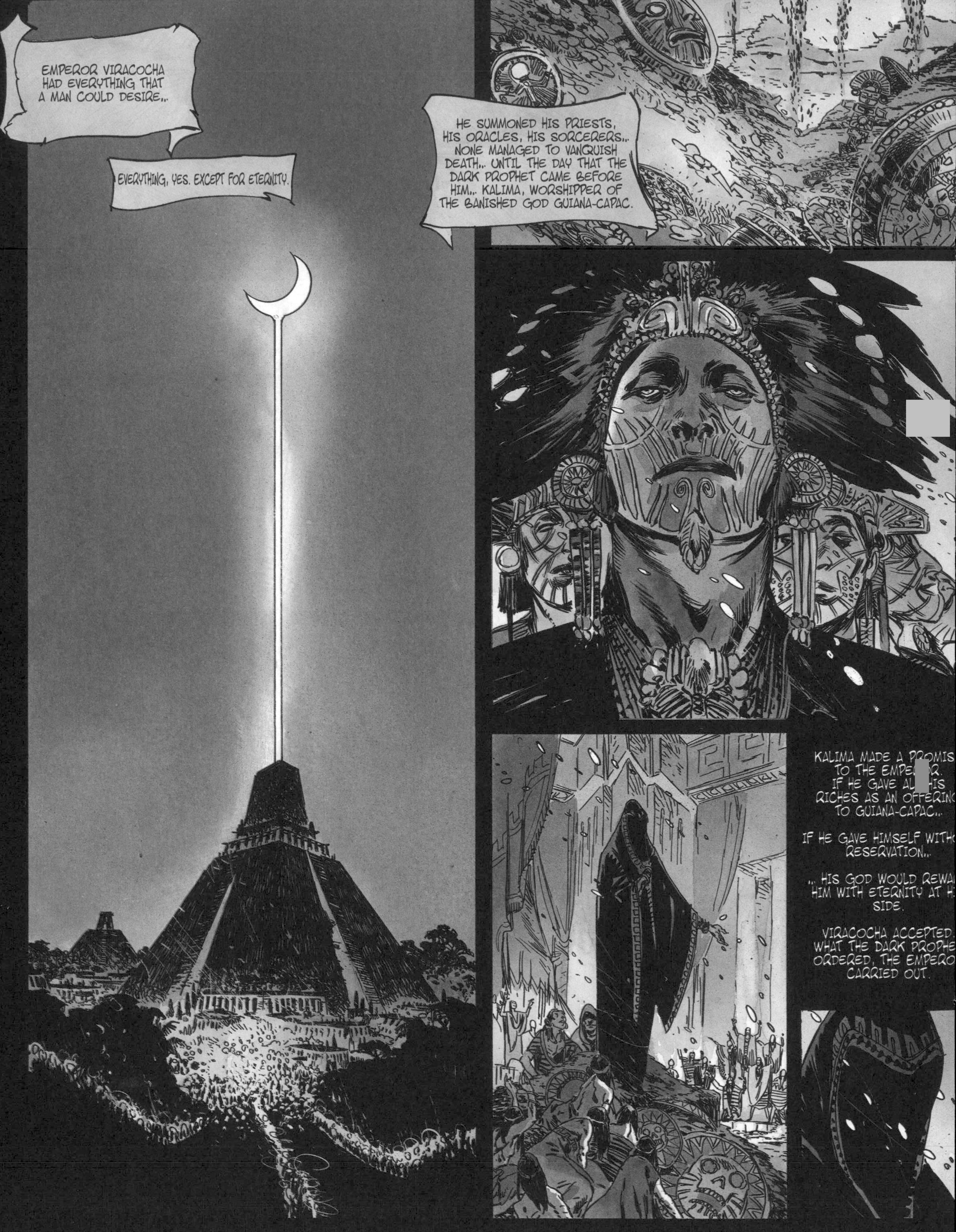
EMPEROR VIRACOCHA HAD EVERYTHING THAT A MAN COULD DESIRE...
EVERYTHING, YES. EXCEPT FOR ETERNITY.
HE SUMMONED HIS PRIESTS, HIS ORACLES, HIS SORCERERS... NONE MANAGED TO VANQUISH DEATH... UNTIL THE DAY THAT THE DARK PROPHET CAME BEFORE HIM... KALIMA, WORSHIPPER OF THE BANISHED GOD GUIANA-CAPAC.
KALIMA MADE A PROMIS TO THE EMPE OR. IF HE GAVE AL HIS RICHES AS AN OFFERING TO GUIANA-CAPAC...
IF HE GAVE HIMSELF WITHO RESERVATION...
... HIS GOD WOULD REWA HIM WITH ETERNITY AT H SIDE.
VIRACOCHA ACCEPTED. WHAT THE DARK PROPHE ORDERED, THE EMPERO CARRIED OUT.

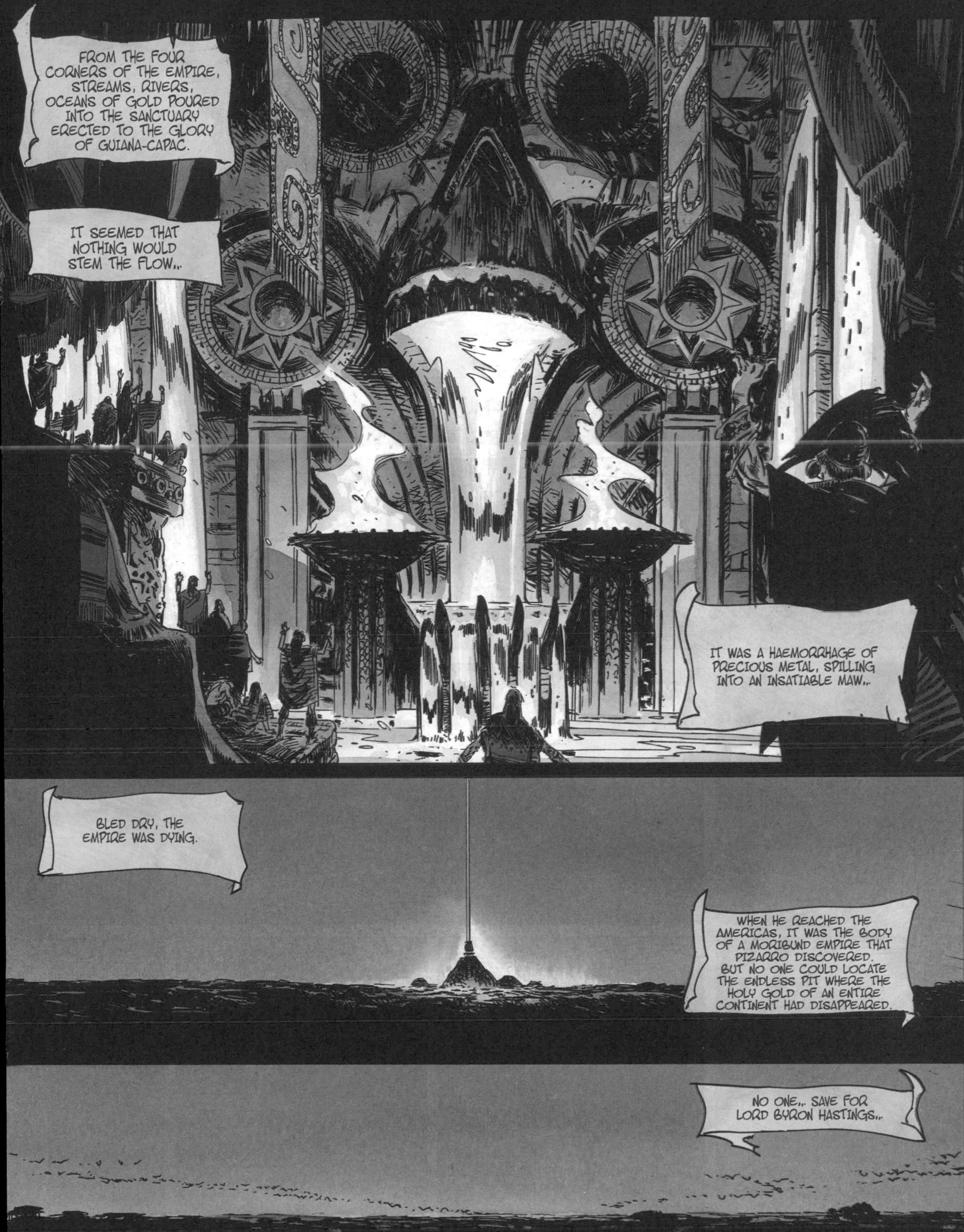
FROM THE FOUR CORNERS OF THE EMPIRE, STREAMS, RIVERS, OCEANS OF GOLD POURED INTO THE SANCTUARY ERECTED TO THE GLORY OF GUIANA-CAPAC.
IT SEEMED THAT NOTHING WOULD STEM THE FLOW...
IT WAS A HAEMORRHAGE OF PRECIOUS METAL, SPILLING INTO AN INSATIABLE MAW...
BLED DRY, THE EMPIRE WAS DYING.
WHEN HE REACHED THE AMERICAS, IT WAS THE BODY OF A MORIBUND EMPIRE THAT PIZARRO DISCOVERED. BUT NO ONE COULD LOCATE THE ENDLESS PIT WHERE THE HOLY GOLD OF AN ENTIRE CONTINENT HAD DISAPPEARED.
NO ONE... SAVE FOR LORD BYRON HASTINGS...

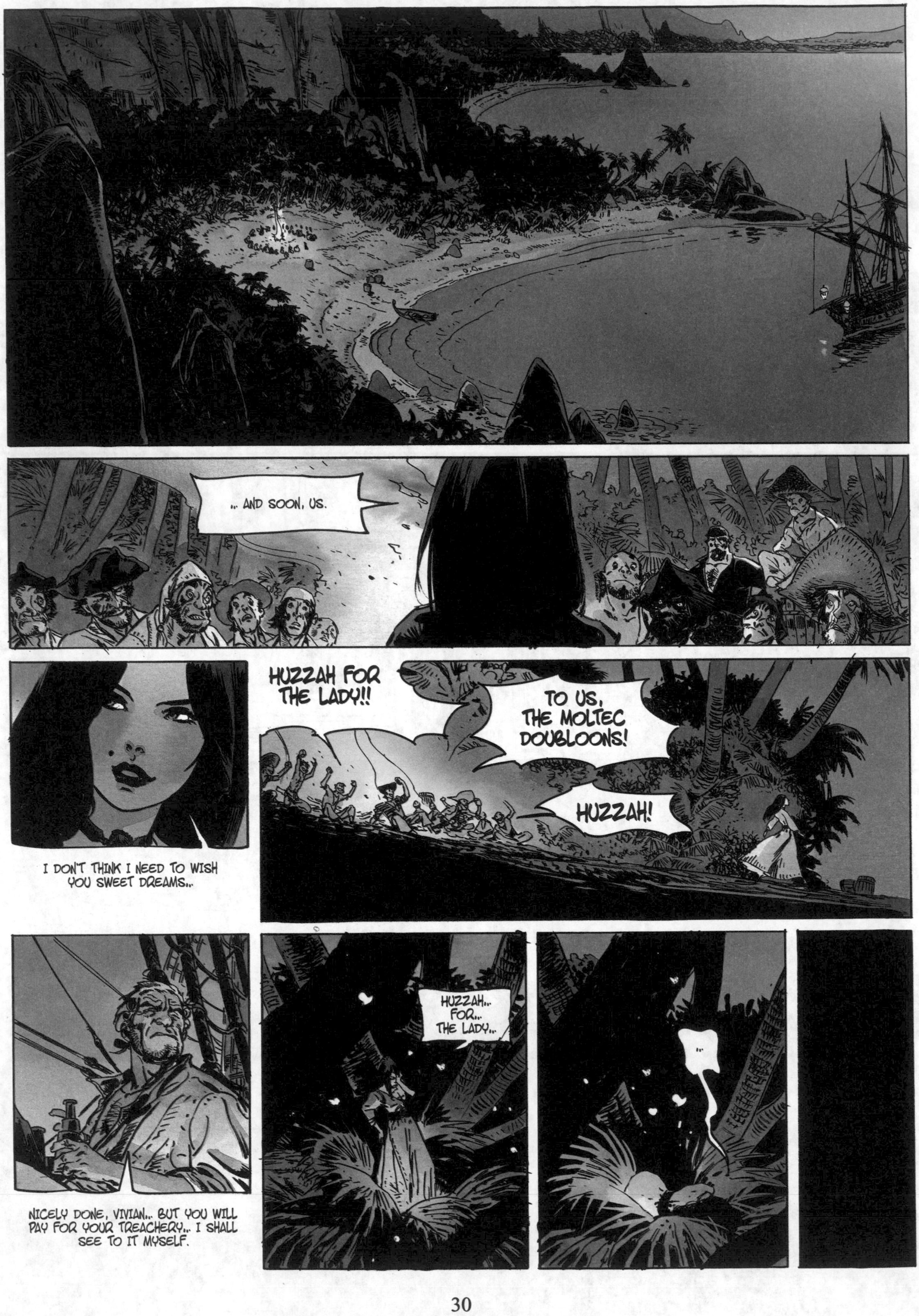
.. AND SOON, US.
I DON'T THINK I NEED TO WISH YOU SWEET DREAMS..
HUZZAH FOR THE LADY!!
TO US, THE MOLTEC DOUBLOONS!
HUZZAH!
NICELY DONE, VIVIAN.. BUT YOU WILL PAY FOR YOUR TREACHERY.. I SHALL SEE TO IT MYSELF.
HUZZAH.. FOR.. THE LADY..
..

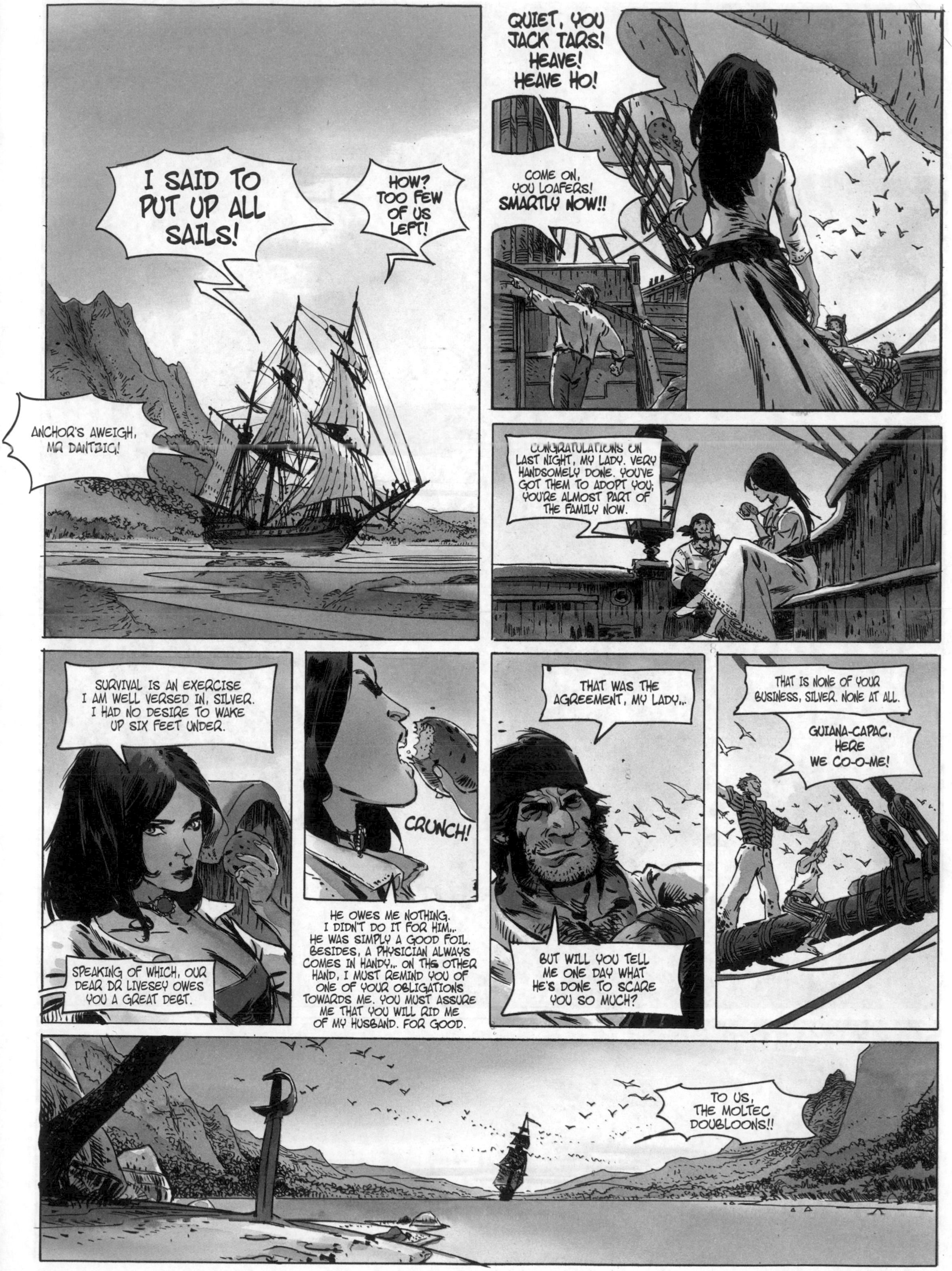

I SAID TO PUT UP ALL SAILS!
HOW? TOO FEW OF US LEFT!
ANCHOR'S AWEIGH, MR DANTZIG!
QUIET, YOU JACK TARS! HEAVE! HEAVE HO!
COME ON, YOU LOAFERS! SMARTLY NOW!!
CONGRATULATIONS ON LAST NIGHT, MY LADY. VERY HANDSOMELY DONE. YOU'VE GOT THEM TO ADOPT YOU; YOU'RE ALMOST PART OF THE FAMILY NOW.
SURVIVAL IS AN EXERCISE I AM WELL VERSED IN, SILVER. I HAD NO DESIRE TO WAKE UP SIX FEET UNDER.
SPEAKING OF WHICH, OUR DEAR DR LIVESEY OWES YOU A GREAT DEBT.
CRUNCH!
HE OWES ME NOTHING. I DIDN'T DO IT FOR HIM.. HE WAS SIMPLY A GOOD FOIL. BESIDES, A PHYSICIAN ALWAYS COMES IN HANDY.. ON THE OTHER HAND, I MUST REMIND YOU OF ONE OF YOUR OBLIGATIONS TOWARDS ME. YOU MUST ASSURE ME THAT YOU WILL RID ME OF MY HUSBAND. FOR GOOD.
THAT WAS THE AGREEMENT, MY LADY..
BUT WILL YOU TELL ME ONE DAY WHAT HE'S DONE TO SCARE YOU SO MUCH?
THAT IS NONE OF YOUR BUSINESS, SILVER. NONE AT ALL.
GUIANA-CAPAC, HERE WE CO-O-ME!
TO US, THE MOLTEC DOUBLOONS!!

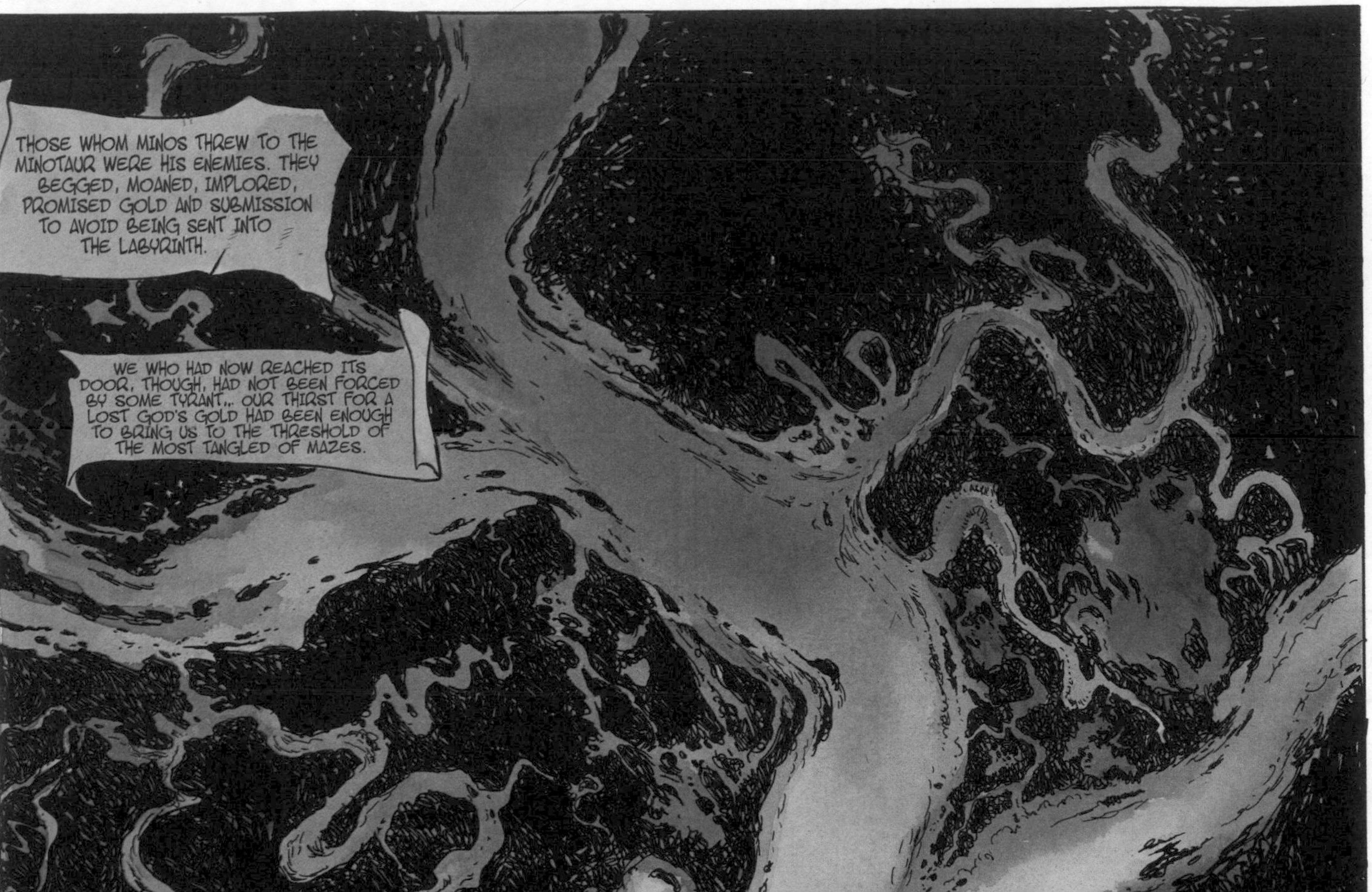
THOSE WHOM MINOS THREW TO THE MINOTAUR WERE HIS ENEMIES. THEY BEGGED, MOANED, IMPLORED, PROMISED GOLD AND SUBMISSION TO AVOID BEING SENT INTO THE LABYRINTH.
WE WHO HAD NOW REACHED ITS DOOR, THOUGH, HAD NOT BEEN FORCED BY SOME TYRANT... OUR THIRST FOR A LOST GOD'S GOLD HAD BEEN ENOUGH TO BRING US TO THE THRESHOLD OF THE MOST TANGLED OF MAZES.
AND I, MODERN DAEDALUS, WAS ITS ARCHITECT.
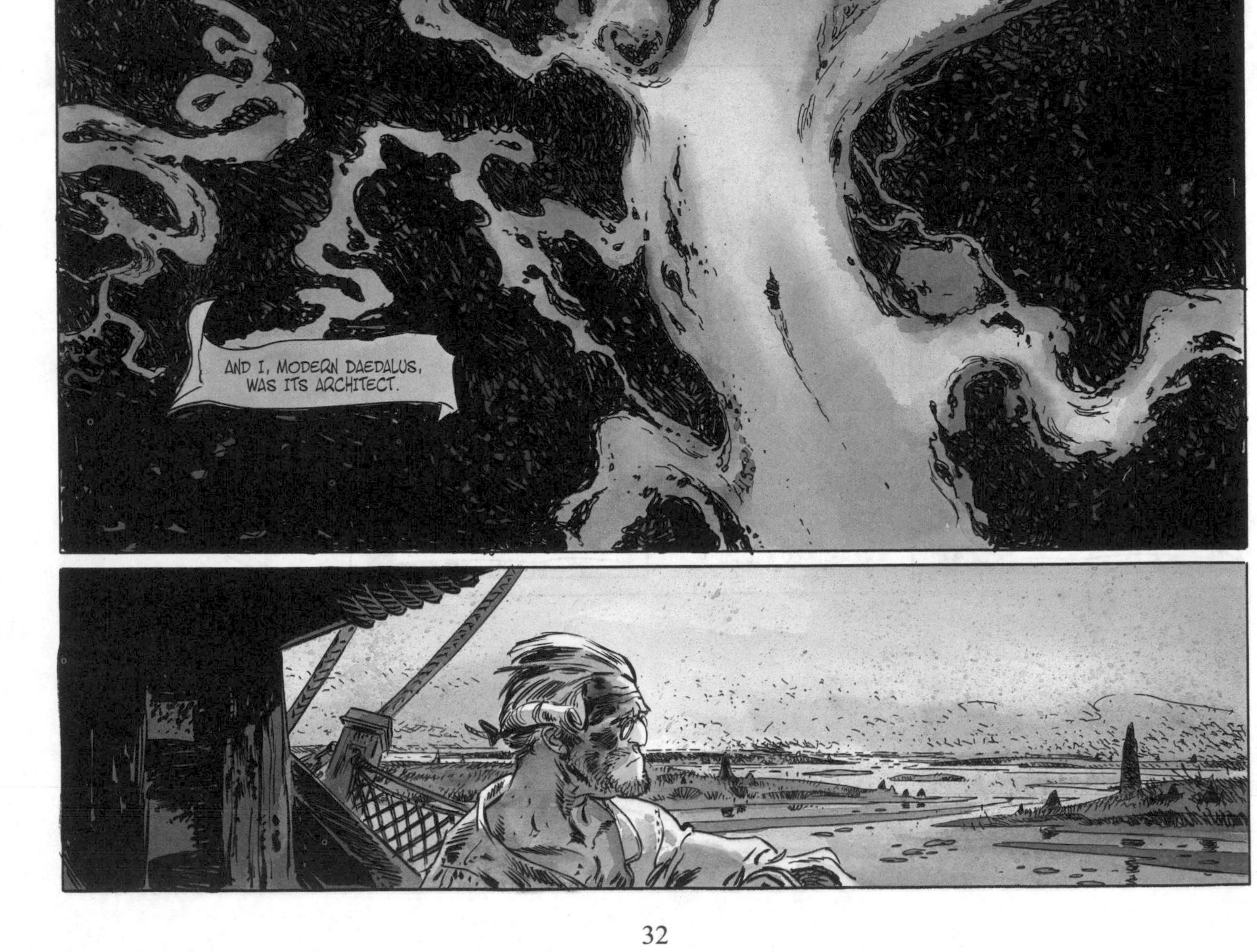

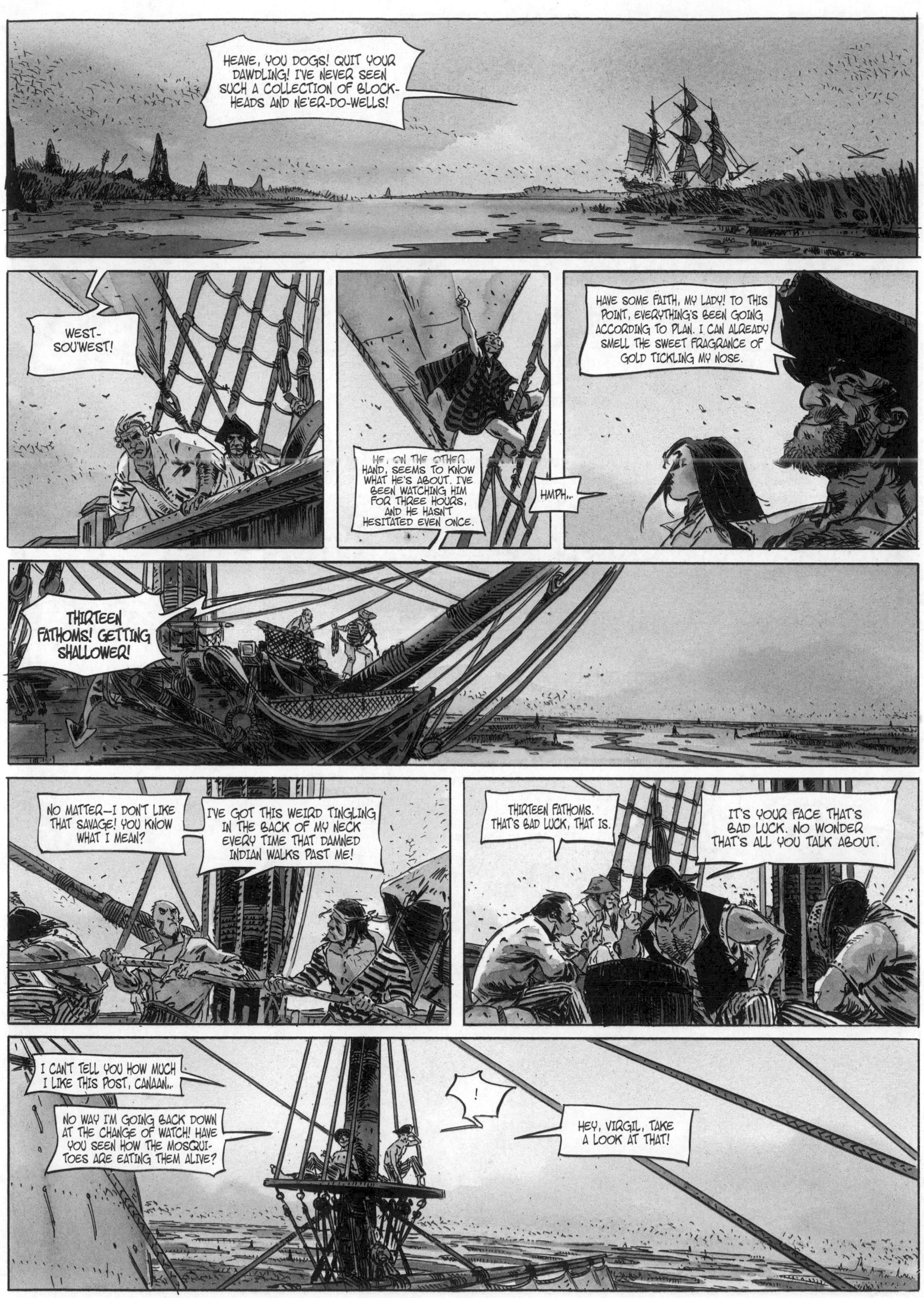
HEAVE, YOU DOGS! QUIT YOUR DAWDLING! I'VE NEVER SEEN SUCH A COLLECTION OF BLOCK-HEADS AND NE'ER-DO-WELLS!
WEST-SOU'WEST!
HE, ON THE OTHER HAND, SEEMS TO KNOW WHAT HE'S ABOUT. I'VE BEEN WATCHING HIM FOR THREE HOURS, AND HE HASN'T HESITATED EVEN ONCE.
HMPH...
HAVE SOME FAITH, MY LADY! TO THIS POINT, EVERYTHING'S BEEN GOING ACCORDING TO PLAN. I CAN ALREADY SMELL THE SWEET FRAGRANCE OF GOLD TICKLING MY NOSE.
THIRTEEN FATHOMS! GETTING SHALLOWER!
NO MATTER—I DON'T LIKE THAT SAVAGE! YOU KNOW WHAT I MEAN?
I'VE GOT THIS WEIRD TINGLING IN THE BACK OF MY NECK EVERY TIME THAT DAMNED INDIAN WALKS PAST ME!
THIRTEEN FATHOMS. THAT'S BAD LUCK, THAT IS.
IT'S YOUR FACE THAT'S BAD LUCK. NO WONDER THAT'S ALL YOU TALK ABOUT.
I CAN'T TELL YOU HOW MUCH I LIKE THIS POST, CANAAN...
NO WAY I'M GOING BACK DOWN AT THE CHANGE OF WATCH! HAVE YOU SEEN HOW THE MOSQUI-TOES ARE EATING THEM ALIVE?
!
HEY, VIRGIL, TAKE A LOOK AT THAT!

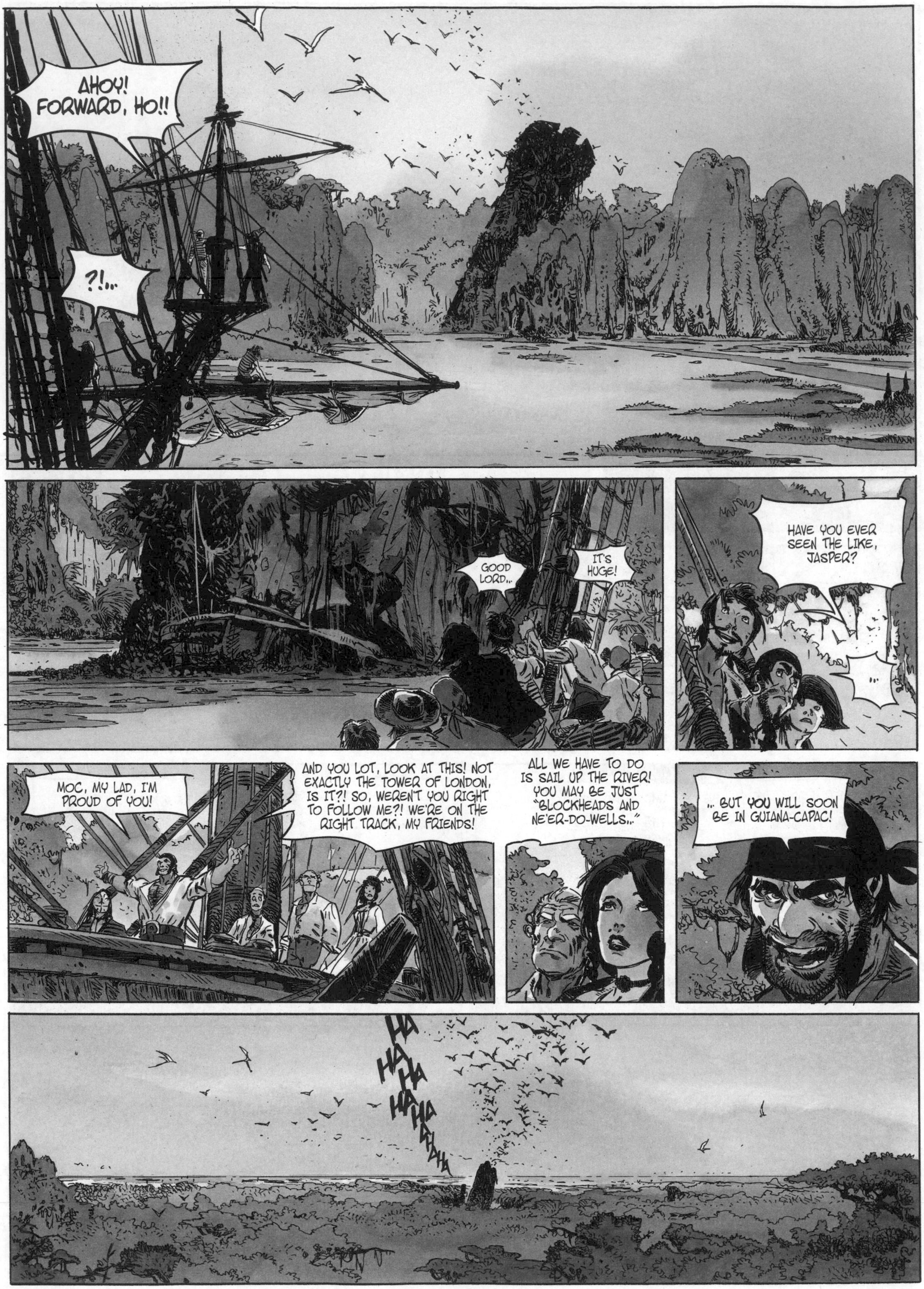
AHOY! FORWARD, HO!!
?!..
GOOD LORD...
IT'S HUGE!
HAVE YOU EVER SEEN THE LIKE, JASPER?
...
MOC, MY LAD, I'M PROUD OF YOU!
AND YOU LOT, LOOK AT THIS! NOT EXACTLY THE TOWER OF LONDON, IS IT?! SO, WEREN'T YOU RIGHT TO FOLLOW ME?! WE'RE ON THE RIGHT TRACK, MY FRIENDS!
ALL WE HAVE TO DO IS SAIL UP THE RIVER! YOU MAY BE JUST "BLOCKHEADS AND NE'ER-DO-WELLS..."
.. BUT YOU WILL SOON BE IN GUIANA-CAPAC!
HA HA HA HA HA HA HAHA

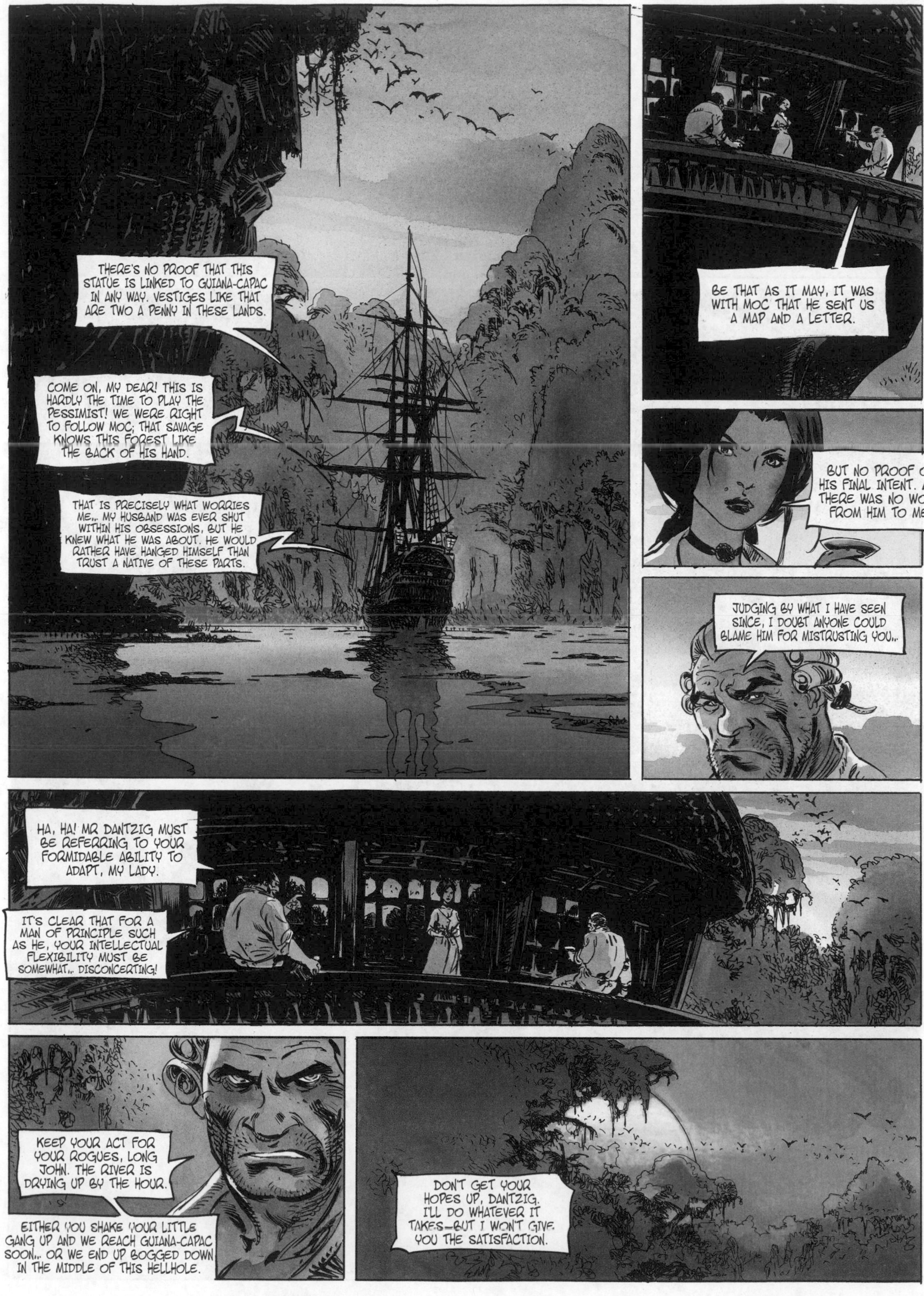
THERE'S NO PROOF THAT THIS STATUE IS LINKED TO GUIANA-CAPAC IN ANY WAY. VESTIGES LIKE THAT ARE TWO A PENNY IN THESE LANDS.
COME ON, MY DEAR! THIS IS HARDLY THE TIME TO PLAY THE PESSIMIST! WE WERE RIGHT TO FOLLOW MOC; THAT SAVAGE KNOWS THIS FOREST LIKE THE BACK OF HIS HAND.
THAT IS PRECISELY WHAT WORRIES ME... MY HUSBAND WAS EVER SHUT WITHIN HIS OBSESSIONS, BUT HE KNEW WHAT HE WAS ABOUT. HE WOULD RATHER HAVE HANGED HIMSELF THAN TRUST A NATIVE OF THESE PARTS.
BE THAT AS IT MAY, IT WAS WITH MOC THAT HE SENT US A MAP AND A LETTER.
BUT NO PROOF OF HIS FINAL INTENT. AND THERE WAS NO WORD FROM HIM TO ME.
JUDGING BY WHAT I HAVE SEEN SINCE, I DOUBT ANYONE COULD BLAME HIM FOR MISTRUSTING YOU...
HA, HA! MR DANTZIG MUST BE REFERRING TO YOUR FORMIDABLE ABILITY TO ADAPT, MY LADY.
IT'S CLEAR THAT FOR A MAN OF PRINCIPLE SUCH AS HE, YOUR INTELLECTUAL FLEXIBILITY MUST BE SOMEWHAT... DISCONCERTING!
KEEP YOUR ACT FOR YOUR ROGUES, LONG JOHN. THE RIVER IS DRYING UP BY THE HOUR.
EITHER YOU SHAKE YOUR LITTLE GANG UP AND WE REACH GUIANA-CAPAC SOON... OR WE END UP BOGGED DOWN IN THE MIDDLE OF THIS HELLHOLE.
DON'T GET YOUR HOPES UP, DANTZIG. I'LL DO WHATEVER IT TAKES—BUT I WON'T GIVE YOU THE SATISFACTION.

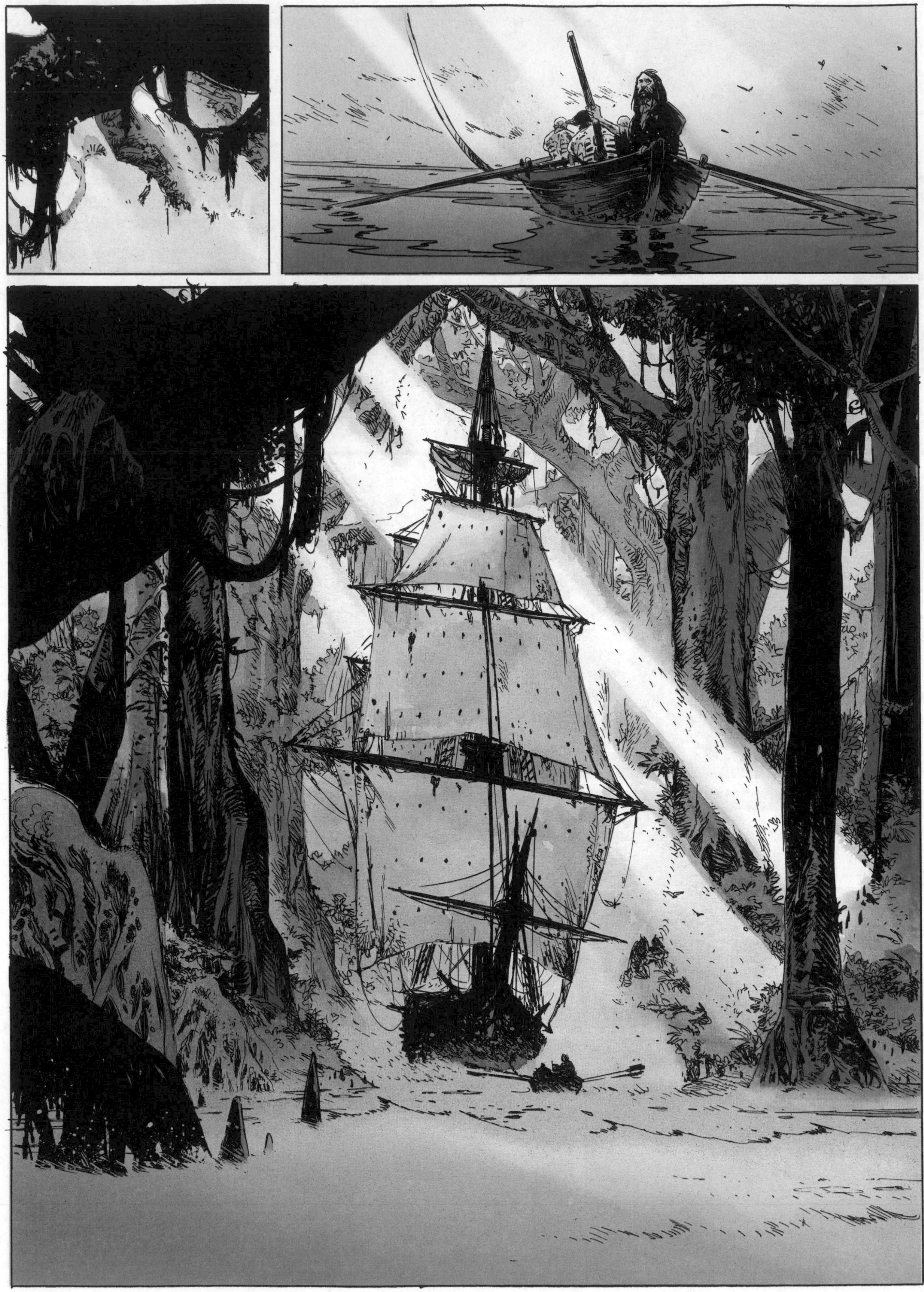

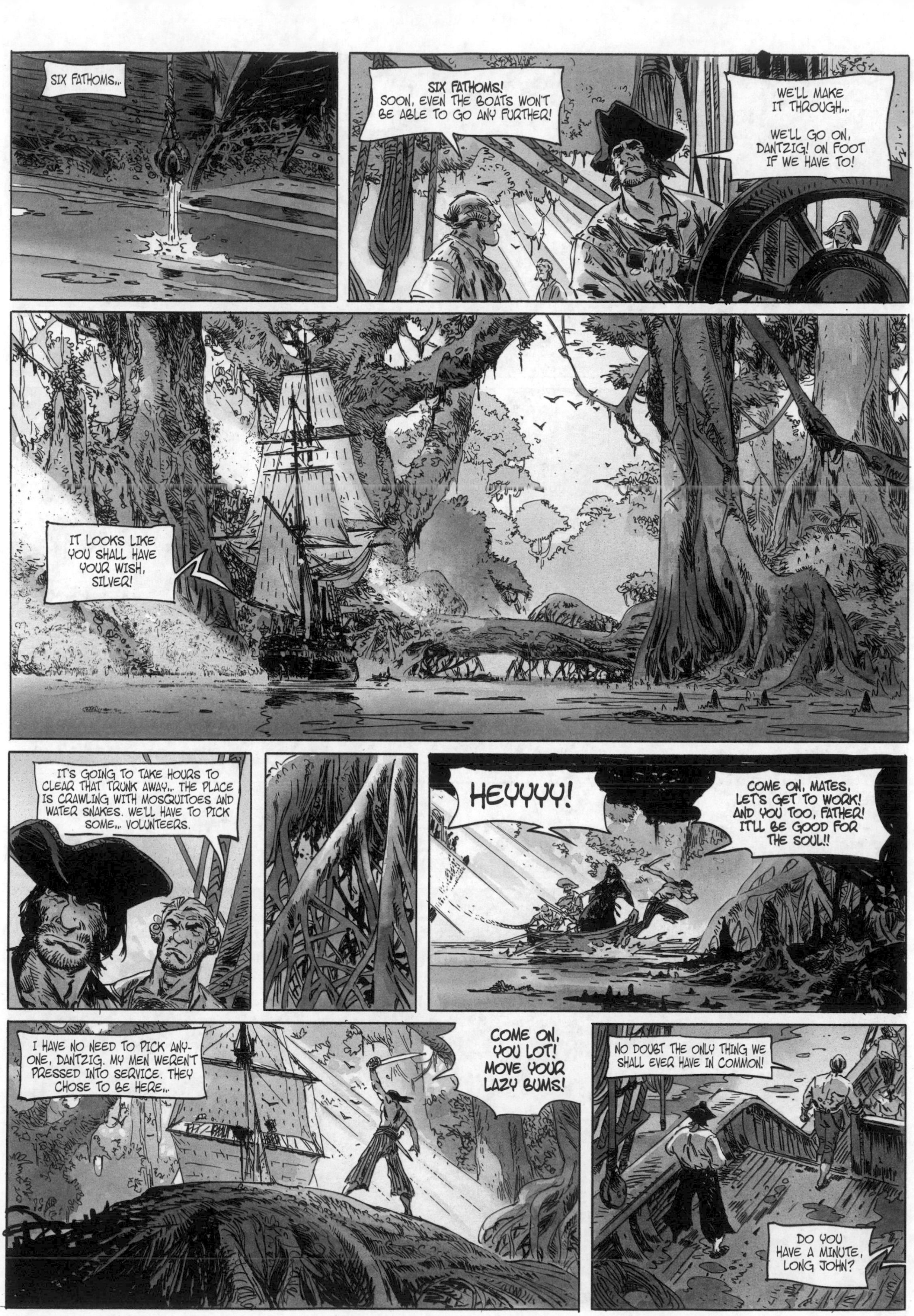

SIX FATHOMS...
SIX FATHOMS! SOON, EVEN THE BOATS WON'T BE ABLE TO GO ANY FURTHER!
WE'LL MAKE IT THROUGH... WE'LL GO ON, DANTZIG! ON FOOT IF WE HAVE TO!
IT LOOKS LIKE YOU SHALL HAVE YOUR WISH, SILVER!
IT'S GOING TO TAKE HOURS TO CLEAR THAT TRUNK AWAY... THE PLACE IS CRAWLING WITH MOSQUITOES AND WATER SNAKES. WE'LL HAVE TO PICK SOME... VOLUNTEERS.
HEYYYY!
COME ON, MATES, LET'S GET TO WORK! AND YOU TOO, FATHER! IT'LL BE GOOD FOR THE SOUL!!
I HAVE NO NEED TO PICK ANY-ONE, DANTZIG. MY MEN WEREN'T PRESSED INTO SERVICE. THEY CHOSE TO BE HERE...
COME ON, YOU LOT! MOVE YOUR LAZY BUMS!
NO DOUBT THE ONLY THING WE SHALL EVER HAVE IN COMMON!
DO YOU HAVE A MINUTE, LONG JOHN?

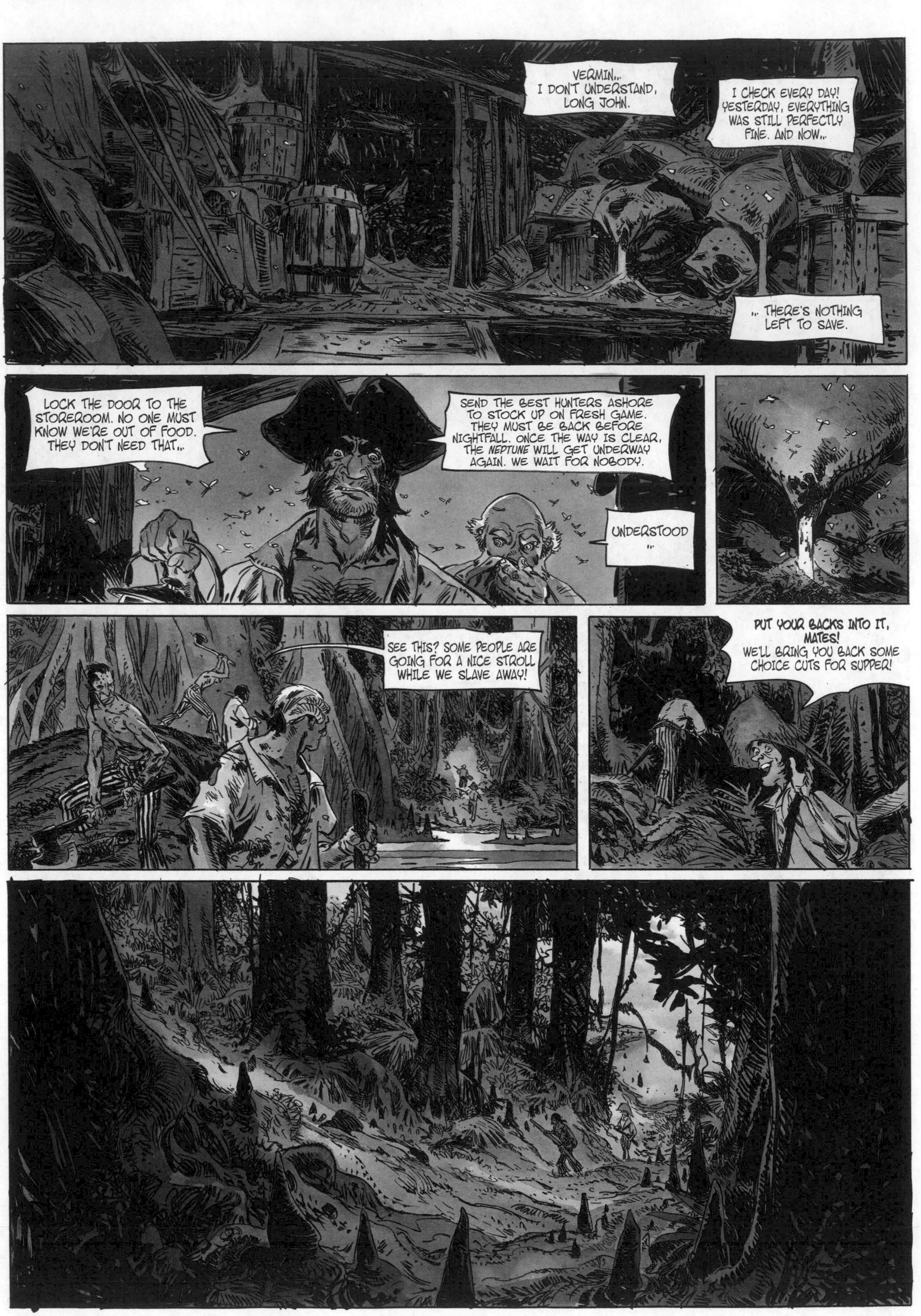
VERMIN... I DON'T UNDERSTAND, LONG JOHN.
I CHECK EVERY DAY! YESTERDAY, EVERYTHING WAS STILL PERFECTLY FINE. AND NOW...
... THERE'S NOTHING LEFT TO SAVE.
LOCK THE DOOR TO THE STOREROOM. NO ONE MUST KNOW WE'RE OUT OF FOOD. THEY DON'T NEED THAT...
SEND THE BEST HUNTERS ASHORE TO STOCK UP ON FRESH GAME. THEY MUST BE BACK BEFORE NIGHTFALL. ONCE THE WAY IS CLEAR, THE NEPTUNE WILL GET UNDERWAY AGAIN. WE WAIT FOR NOBODY.
UNDERSTOOD ...
SEE THIS? SOME PEOPLE ARE GOING FOR A NICE STROLL WHILE WE SLAVE AWAY!
PUT YOUR BACKS INTO IT, MATES! WE'LL BRING YOU BACK SOME CHOICE CUTS FOR SUPPER!

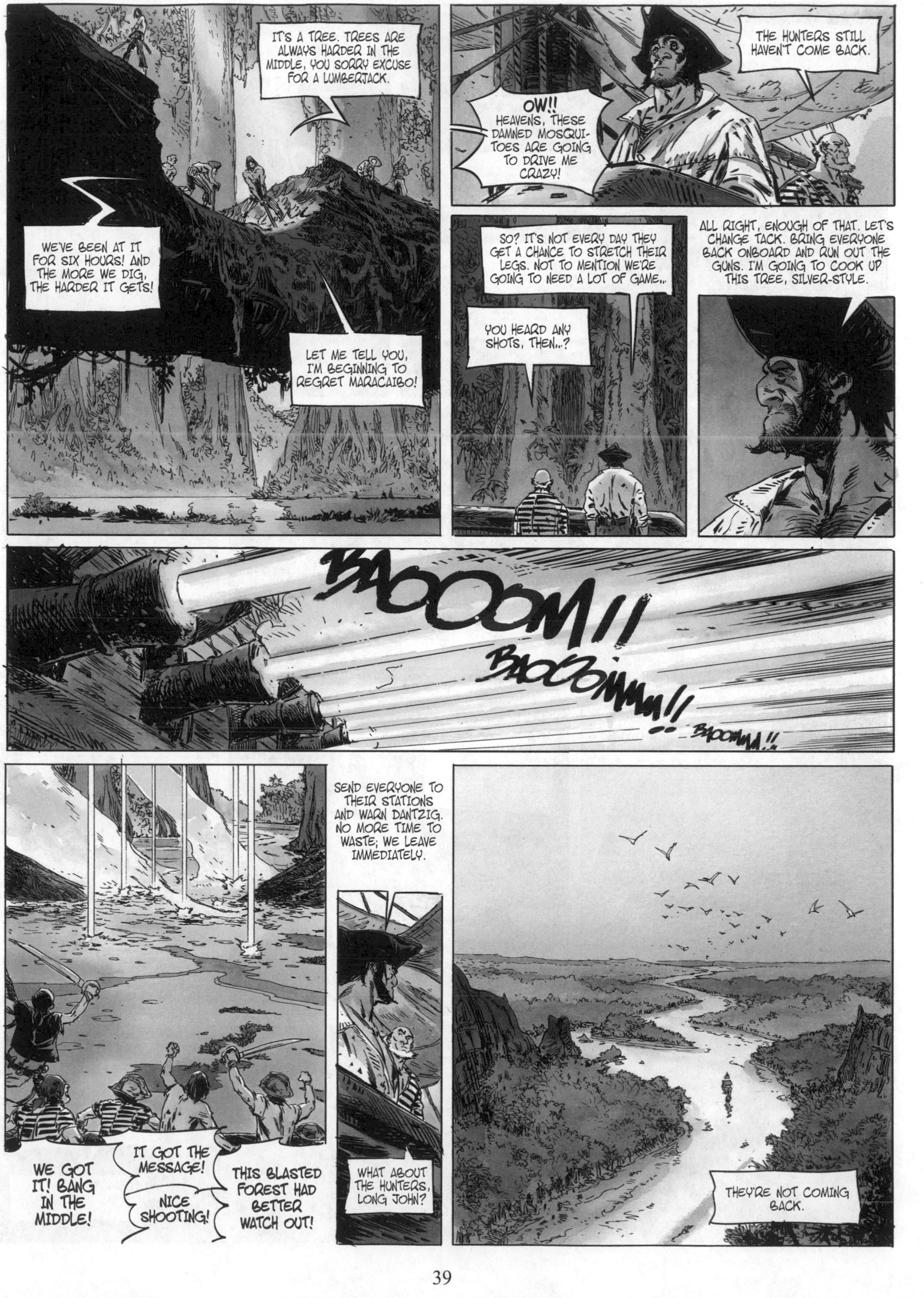
IT'S A TREE. TREES ARE ALWAYS HARDER IN THE MIDDLE, YOU SORRY EXCUSE FOR A LUMBERJACK.
WE'VE BEEN AT IT FOR SIX HOURS! AND THE MORE WE DIG, THE HARDER IT GETS!
LET ME TELL YOU, I'M BEGINNING TO REGRET MARACAIBO!
THE HUNTERS STILL HAVEN'T COME BACK.
OW!! HEAVENS, THESE DAMNED MOSQUITOES ARE GOING TO DRIVE ME CRAZY!
SO? IT'S NOT EVERY DAY THEY GET A CHANCE TO STRETCH THEIR LEGS. NOT TO MENTION WE'RE GOING TO NEED A LOT OF GAME...
YOU HEARD ANY SHOTS, THEN...?
ALL RIGHT, ENOUGH OF THAT. LET'S CHANGE TACK. BRING EVERYONE BACK ONBOARD AND RUN OUT THE GUNS. I'M GOING TO COOK UP THIS TREE, SILVER-STYLE.
BAOOOOM!!
BAOOOMMM!!
BAOOMMM!!
WE GOT IT! BANG IN THE MIDDLE!
IT GOT THE MESSAGE!
NICE SHOOTING!
THIS BLASTED FOREST HAD BETTER WATCH OUT!
SEND EVERYONE TO THEIR STATIONS AND WARN DANTZIG. NO MORE TIME TO WASTE; WE LEAVE IMMEDIATELY.
WHAT ABOUT THE HUNTERS, LONG JOHN?
THEY'RE NOT COMING BACK.

MOC, ANSWER ME. I MUST KNOW.

GUIANA-CAPAC SOON, NEAR...

IT'S LORD HASTINGS I WANT YOU TO TELL ME ABOUT. I TOLD YOU. YOU DON'T HAVE TO BE SCARED OF HIM. YOU CAN TRUST ME. IF YOU'RE AFRAID OF HIM, I SHALL PROTECT YOU.

LORD HASTINGS VERY GOOD MAN, VERY KIND. FRIEND!

YOU LIE!!

SHLAH!

HE THREATENED YOU! HE'S GOT TO YOU SOMEHOW! IT'S OBVIOUS! TELL ME WHAT YOU'RE HIDING! TELL ME WHY YOU PROTECT HIM?!

WELL... DOES YOUR HUSBAND SCARE YOU THAT MUCH, MY LADY?

?!!

GO ON, MOC, SCARPER...

YOU...

YOU JUST DON'T KNOW HIM.

ON THE OTHER HAND, I'M STARTING TO KNOW YOU... AND I'VE NEVER SEEN YOU BACK DOWN OR HESITATE.

ALWAYS SAILING AGAINST THE WIND. EVEN WHEN THE STRONGEST OF MY LADS WOULD HAVE GIVEN UP!

LOOK AT YOU. YOU'RE SWEATING. YOU'RE WHITE AS A SHEET. I CANNOT BELIEVE THAT A MAN, WHOEVER HE IS, COULD FRIGHTEN YOU THIS MUCH.

TAKE MY WORD FOR IT, MY LADY. IT'S NOT A MAN YOU'RE AFRAID OF. IT'S SOMETHING ELSE.

I PROMISED I'D TAKE CARE OF YOUR HUSBAND AND I WILL. BUT I SERIOUSLY DOUBT THAT'LL MAKE YOUR PROBLEM GO AWAY.

CHANCES ARE, ONLY YOU CAN DO THAT... THINK ON IT.

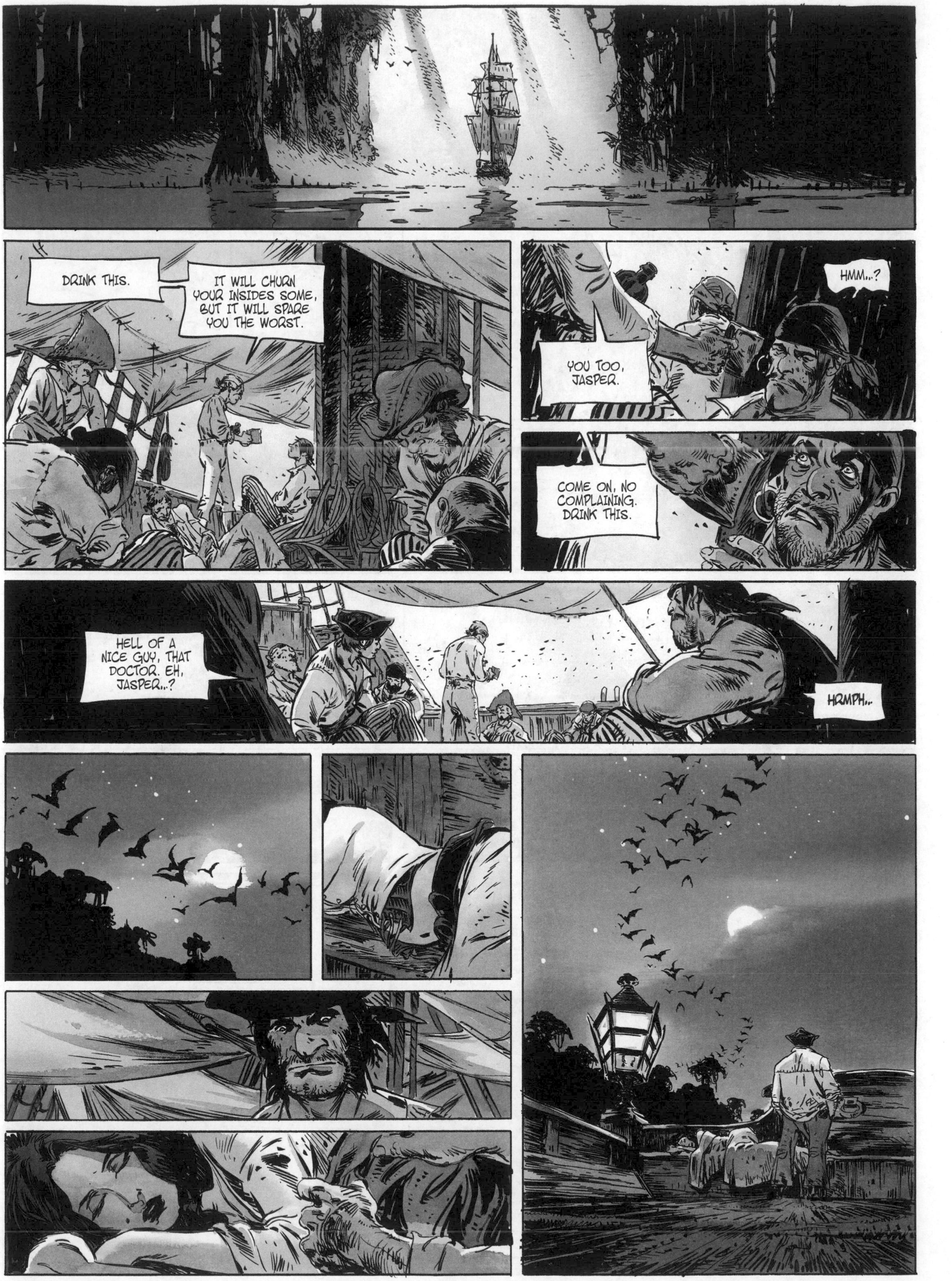

DRINK THIS.
IT WILL CHURN YOUR INSIDES SOME, BUT IT WILL SPARE YOU THE WORST.
HMM...?
YOU TOO, JASPER.
COME ON, NO COMPLAINING. DRINK THIS.
HELL OF A NICE GUY, THAT DOCTOR. EH, JASPER...?
HRMPH...

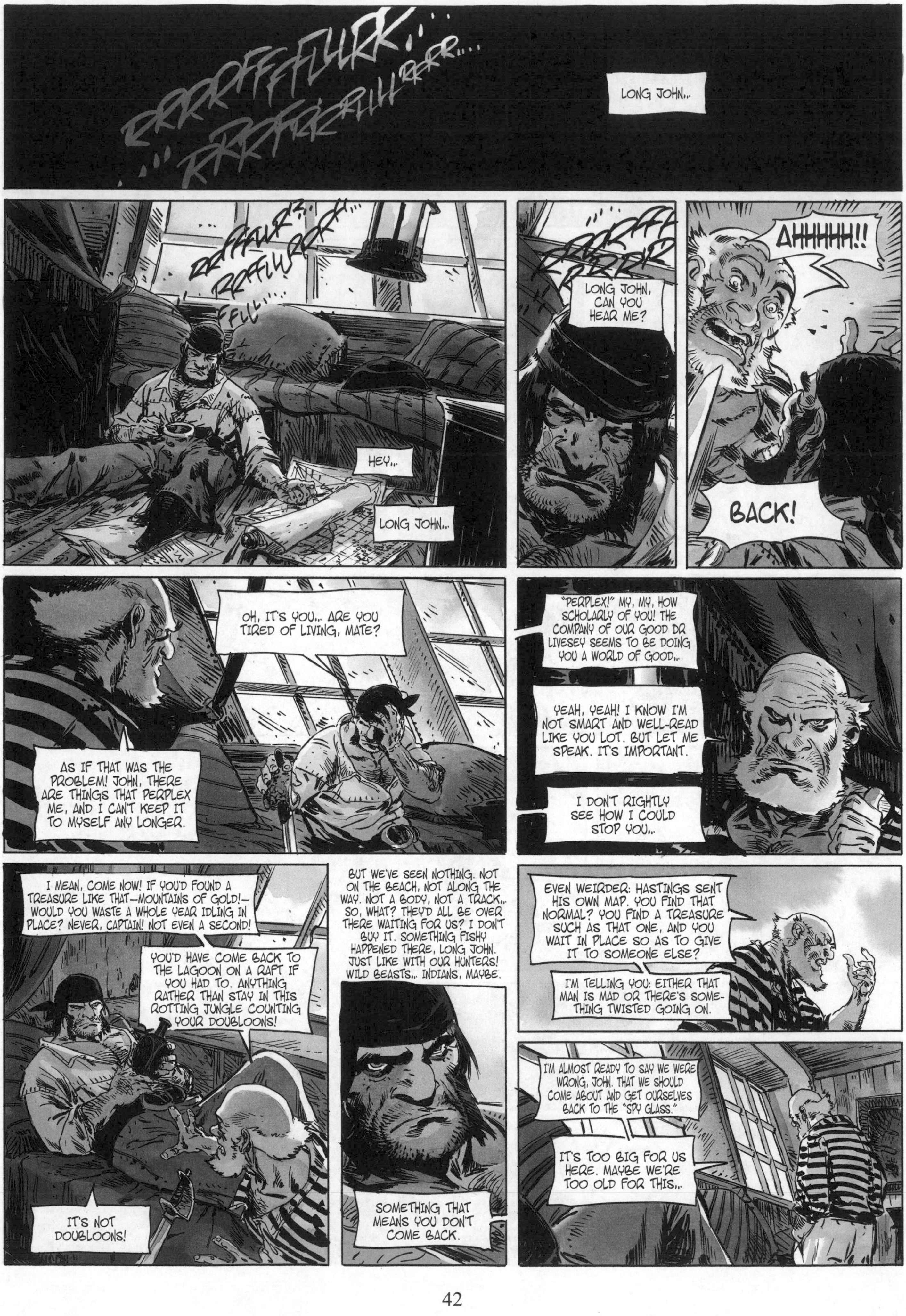

LONG JOHN...
HEY...
LONG JOHN...
LONG JOHN, CAN YOU HEAR ME?
AHHHHH!!
BACK!
OH, IT'S YOU... ARE YOU TIRED OF LIVING, MATE?
AS IF THAT WAS THE PROBLEM! JOHN, THERE ARE THINGS THAT PERPLEX ME, AND I CAN'T KEEP IT TO MYSELF ANY LONGER.
"PERPLEX!" MY, MY, HOW SCHOLARLY OF YOU! THE COMPANY OF OUR GOOD DR LIVESEY SEEMS TO BE DOING YOU A WORLD OF GOOD...
YEAH, YEAH! I KNOW I'M NOT SMART AND WELL-READ LIKE YOU LOT. BUT LET ME SPEAK. IT'S IMPORTANT.
I DON'T RIGHTLY SEE HOW I COULD STOP YOU...
I MEAN, COME NOW! IF YOU'D FOUND A TREASURE LIKE THAT—MOUNTAINS OF GOLD!—WOULD YOU WASTE A WHOLE YEAR IDLING IN PLACE? NEVER, CAPTAIN! NOT EVEN A SECOND!
YOU'D HAVE COME BACK TO THE LAGOON ON A RAFT IF YOU HAD TO. ANYTHING RATHER THAN STAY IN THIS ROTTING JUNGLE COUNTING YOUR DOUBLOONS!
IT'S NOT DOUBLOONS!
BUT WE'VE SEEN NOTHING. NOT ON THE BEACH, NOT ALONG THE WAY. NOT A BODY, NOT A TRACK... SO, WHAT? THEY'D ALL BE OVER THERE WAITING FOR US? I DON'T BUY IT. SOMETHING FISHY HAPPENED THERE, LONG JOHN. JUST LIKE WITH OUR HUNTERS! WILD BEASTS... INDIANS, MAYBE.
SOMETHING THAT MEANS YOU DON'T COME BACK.
EVEN WEIRDER: HASTINGS SENT HIS OWN MAP. YOU FIND THAT NORMAL? YOU FIND A TREASURE SUCH AS THAT ONE, AND YOU WAIT IN PLACE SO AS TO GIVE IT TO SOMEONE ELSE?
I'M TELLING YOU: EITHER THAT MAN IS MAD OR THERE'S SOMETHING TWISTED GOING ON.
I'M ALMOST READY TO SAY WE WERE WRONG, JOHN. THAT WE SHOULD COME ABOUT AND GET OURSELVES BACK TO THE "SPY GLASS."
IT'S TOO BIG FOR US HERE. MAYBE WE'RE TOO OLD FOR THIS...

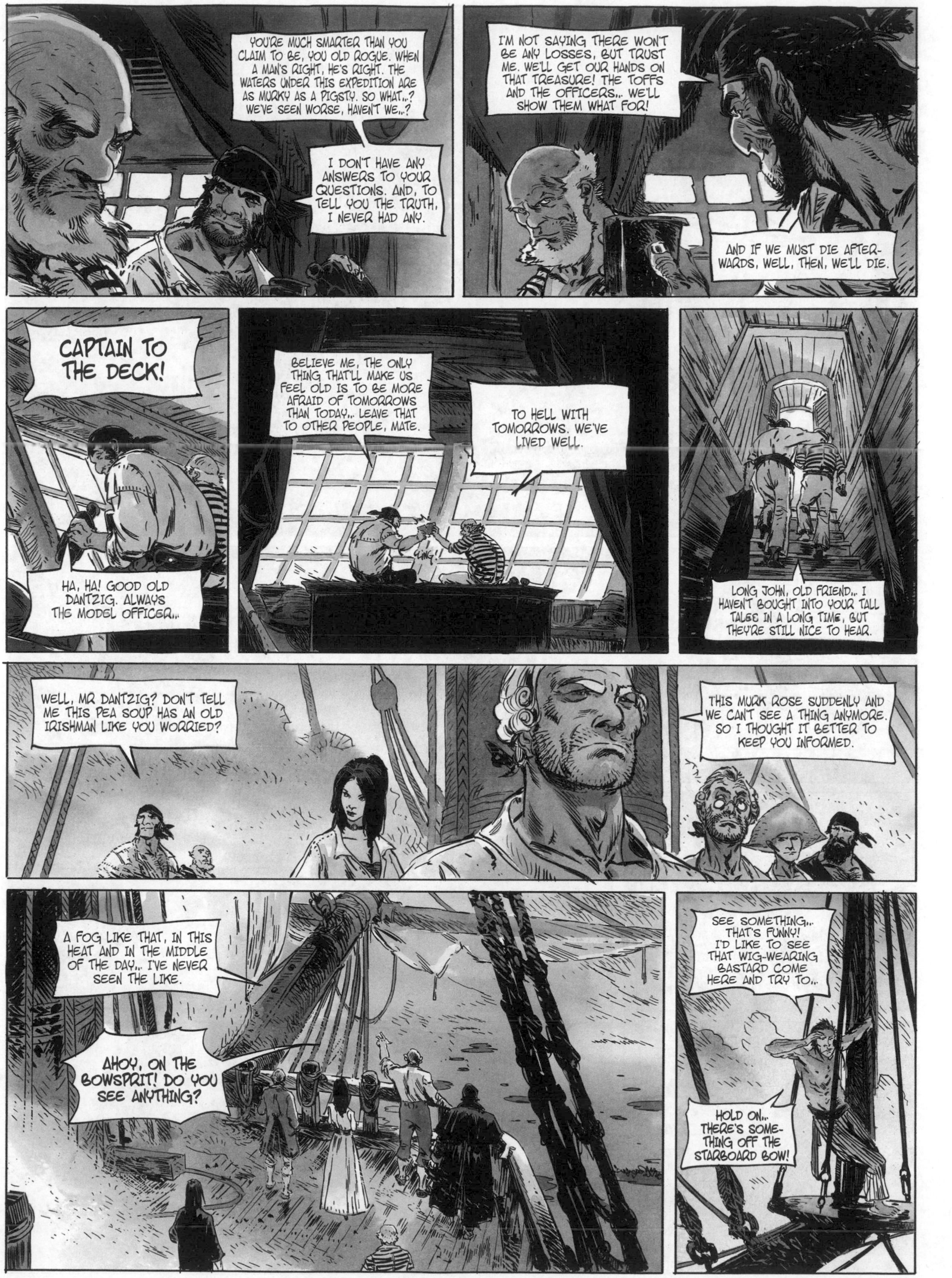

YOU'RE MUCH SMARTER THAN YOU CLAIM TO BE, YOU OLD ROGUE. WHEN A MAN'S RIGHT, HE'S RIGHT. THE WATERS UNDER THIS EXPEDITION ARE AS MURKY AS A PIGSTY. SO WHAT...? WE'VE SEEN WORSE, HAVEN'T WE...?
I DON'T HAVE ANY ANSWERS TO YOUR QUESTIONS. AND, TO TELL YOU THE TRUTH, I NEVER HAD ANY.
I'M NOT SAYING THERE WON'T BE ANY LOSSES, BUT TRUST ME. WE'LL GET OUR HANDS ON THAT TREASURE! THE TOFFS AND THE OFFICERS... WE'LL SHOW THEM WHAT FOR!
AND IF WE MUST DIE AFTER-WARDS, WELL, THEN, WE'LL DIE.
CAPTAIN TO THE DECK!
HA, HA! GOOD OLD DANTZIG. ALWAYS THE MODEL OFFICER...
BELIEVE ME, THE ONLY THING THAT'LL MAKE US FEEL OLD IS TO BE MORE AFRAID OF TOMORROWS THAN TODAY... LEAVE THAT TO OTHER PEOPLE, MATE.
TO HELL WITH TOMORROWS. WE'VE LIVED WELL.
LONG JOHN, OLD FRIEND... I HAVEN'T BOUGHT INTO YOUR TALL TALES IN A LONG TIME, BUT THEY'RE STILL NICE TO HEAR.
WELL, MR DANTZIG? DON'T TELL ME THIS PEA SOUP HAS AN OLD IRISHMAN LIKE YOU WORRIED?
THIS MURK ROSE SUDDENLY AND WE CAN'T SEE A THING ANYMORE. SO I THOUGHT IT BETTER TO KEEP YOU INFORMED.
A FOG LIKE THAT, IN THIS HEAT AND IN THE MIDDLE OF THE DAY... I'VE NEVER SEEN THE LIKE.
AHOY, ON THE BOWSPRIT! DO YOU SEE ANYTHING?
SEE SOMETHING... THAT'S FUNNY! I'D LIKE TO SEE THAT WIG-WEARING BASTARD COME HERE AND TRY TO...
HOLD ON... THERE'S SOME-THING OFF THE STARBOARD BOW!

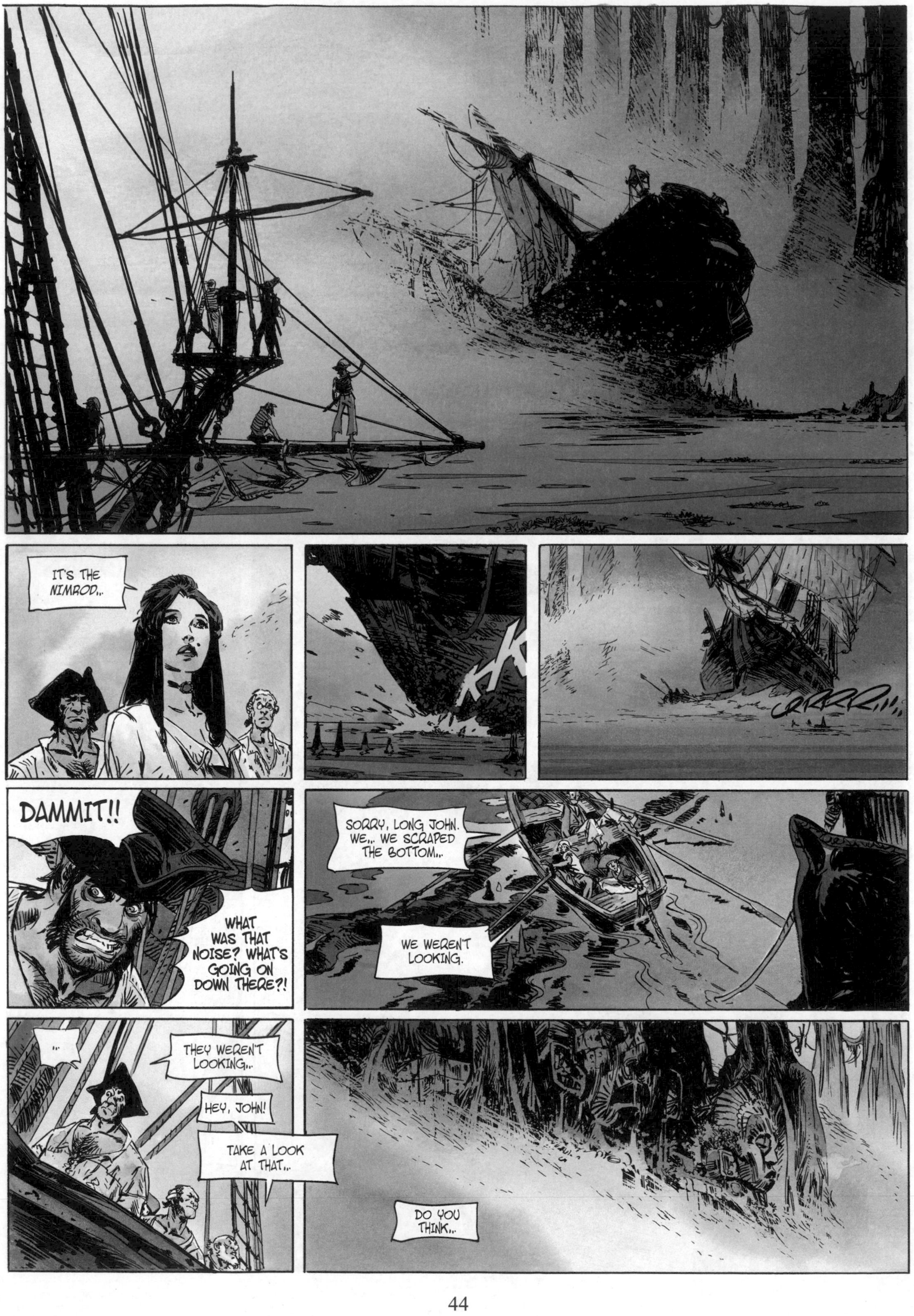
IT'S THE NIMROD...
KK
CRRRR...
DAMMIT!!
WHAT WAS THAT NOISE? WHAT'S GOING ON DOWN THERE?!
SORRY, LONG JOHN. WE... WE SCRAPED THE BOTTOM...
WE WEREN'T LOOKING.
...
THEY WEREN'T LOOKING...
HEY, JOHN!
TAKE A LOOK AT THAT...
DO YOU THINK...

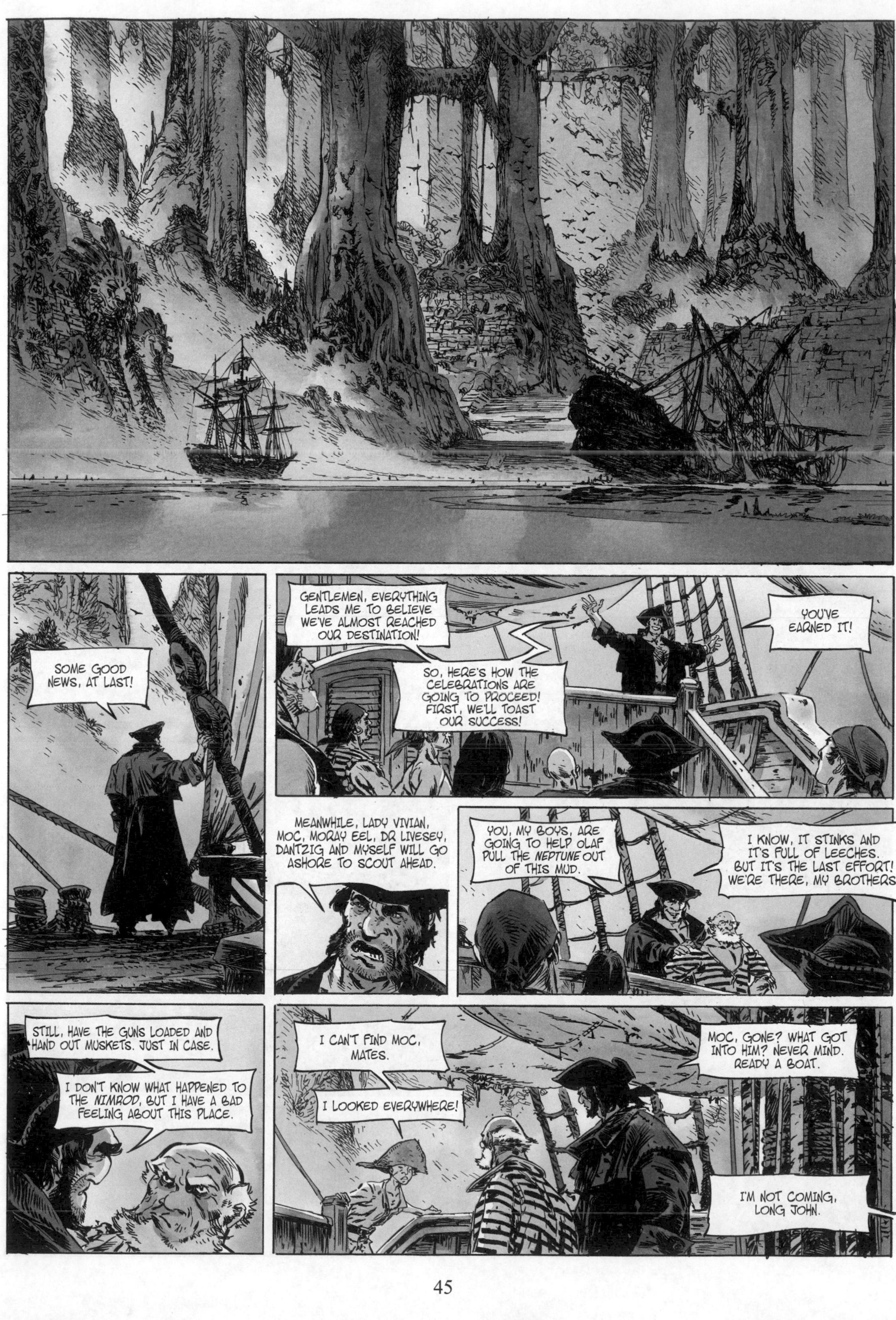
SOME GOOD NEWS, AT LAST!
GENTLEMEN, EVERYTHING LEADS ME TO BELIEVE WE'VE ALMOST REACHED OUR DESTINATION!
SO, HERE'S HOW THE CELEBRATIONS ARE GOING TO PROCEED! FIRST, WE'LL TOAST OUR SUCCESS!
YOU'VE EARNED IT!
MEANWHILE, LADY VIVIAN, MOC, MORAY EEL, DR LIVESEY, DANTZIG AND MYSELF WILL GO ASHORE TO SCOUT AHEAD.
YOU, MY BOYS, ARE GOING TO HELP OLAF PULL THE *NEPTUNE* OUT OF THIS MUD.
I KNOW, IT STINKS AND IT'S FULL OF LEECHES. BUT IT'S THE LAST EFFORT! WE'RE THERE, MY BROTHERS!
STILL, HAVE THE GUNS LOADED AND HAND OUT MUSKETS. JUST IN CASE.
I DON'T KNOW WHAT HAPPENED TO THE *NIMROD*, BUT I HAVE A BAD FEELING ABOUT THIS PLACE.
I CAN'T FIND MOC, MATES.
I LOOKED EVERYWHERE!
MOC, GONE? WHAT GOT INTO HIM? NEVER MIND. READY A BOAT.
I'M NOT COMING, LONG JOHN.

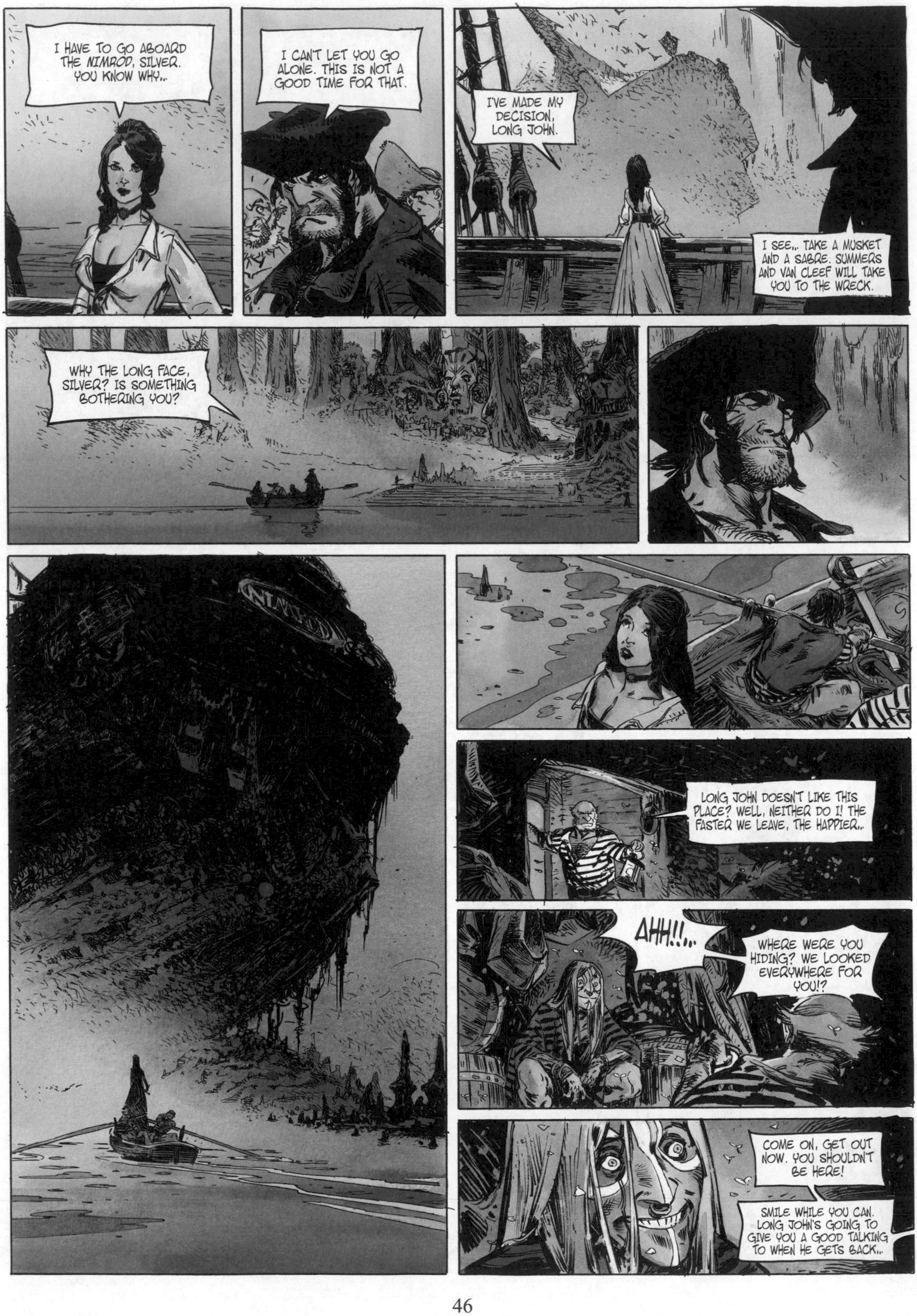

I HAVE TO GO ABOARD THE NIMROD, SILVER. YOU KNOW WHY...
I CAN'T LET YOU GO ALONE. THIS IS NOT A GOOD TIME FOR THAT.
I'VE MADE MY DECISION, LONG JOHN.
I SEE... TAKE A MUSKET AND A SABRE. SUMMERS AND VAN CLEEF WILL TAKE YOU TO THE WRECK.
WHY THE LONG FACE, SILVER? IS SOMETHING BOTHERING YOU?
NIMROD
LONG JOHN DOESN'T LIKE THIS PLACE? WELL, NEITHER DO I! THE FASTER WE LEAVE, THE HAPPIER...
AHH!!...
WHERE WERE YOU HIDING? WE LOOKED EVERYWHERE FOR YOU!?
COME ON, GET OUT NOW. YOU SHOULDN'T BE HERE!
SMILE WHILE YOU CAN. LONG JOHN'S GOING TO GIVE YOU A GOOD TALKING TO WHEN HE GETS BACK...

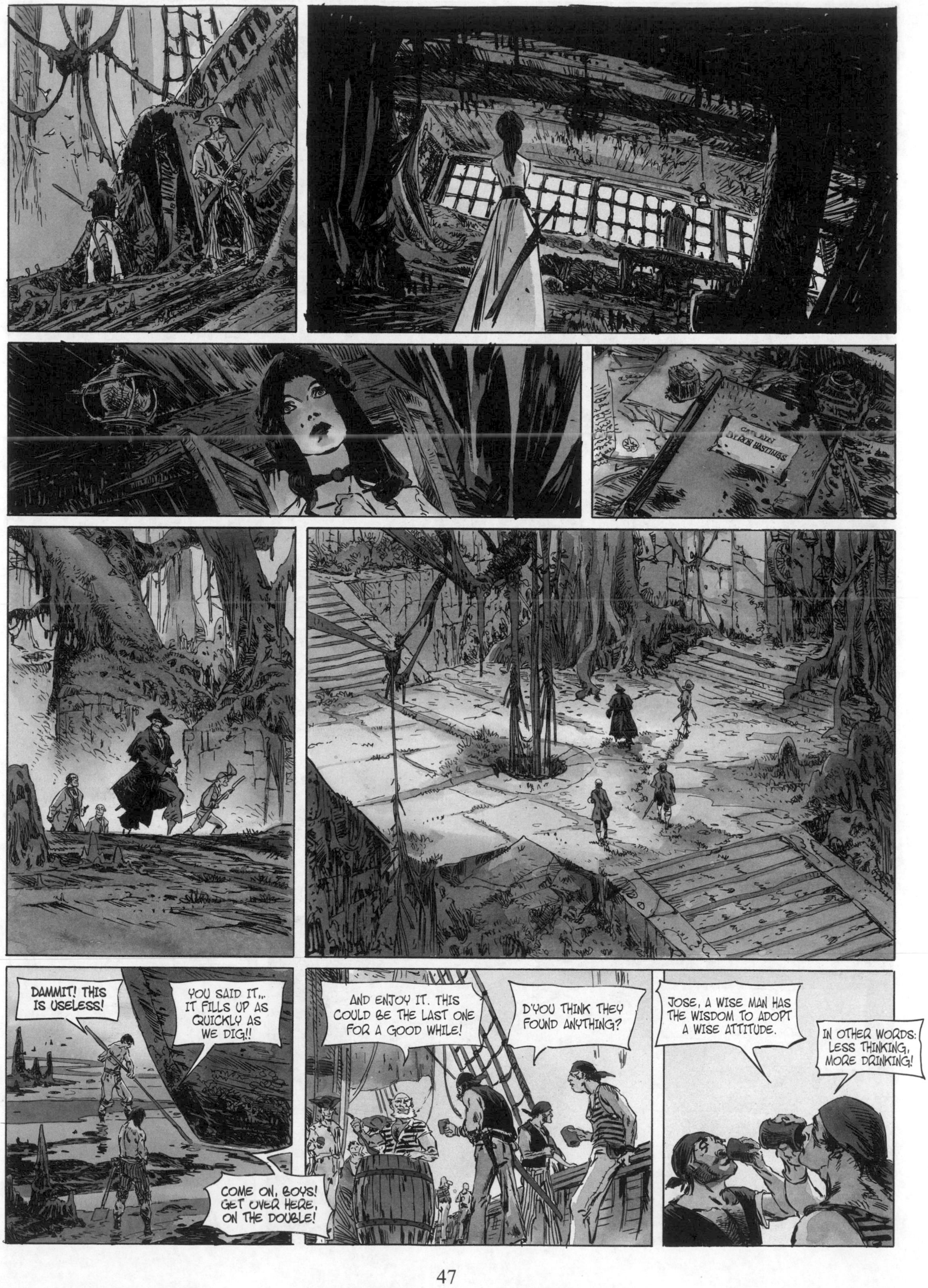
DAMMIT! THIS IS USELESS!
YOU SAID IT... IT FILLS UP AS QUICKLY AS WE DIG!!
COME ON, BOYS! GET OVER HERE, ON THE DOUBLE!
AND ENJOY IT. THIS COULD BE THE LAST ONE FOR A GOOD WHILE!
D'YOU THINK THEY FOUND ANYTHING?
JOSE, A WISE MAN HAS THE WISDOM TO ADOPT A WISE ATTITUDE.
IN OTHER WORDS: LESS THINKING, MORE DRINKING!

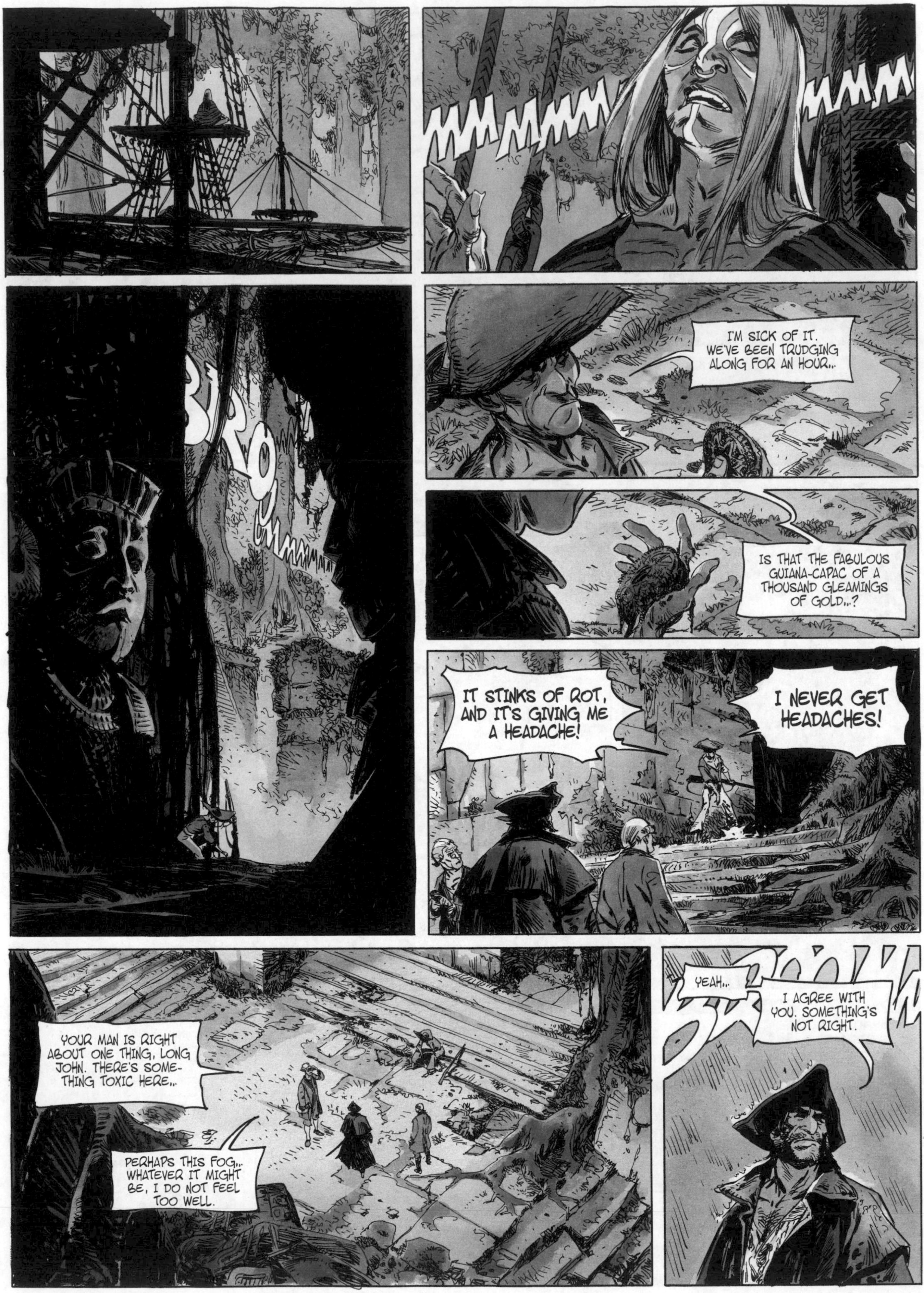
I'M SICK OF IT. WE'VE BEEN TRUDGING ALONG FOR AN HOUR...
IS THAT THE FABULOUS GUIANA-CAPAC OF A THOUSAND GLEAMINGS OF GOLD...?
IT STINKS OF ROT, AND IT'S GIVING ME A HEADACHE!
I NEVER GET HEADACHES!
YOUR MAN IS RIGHT ABOUT ONE THING, LONG JOHN. THERE'S SOME-THING TOXIC HERE...
PERHAPS THIS FOG... WHATEVER IT MIGHT BE, I DO NOT FEEL TOO WELL.
YEAH...
I AGREE WITH YOU. SOMETHING'S NOT RIGHT.

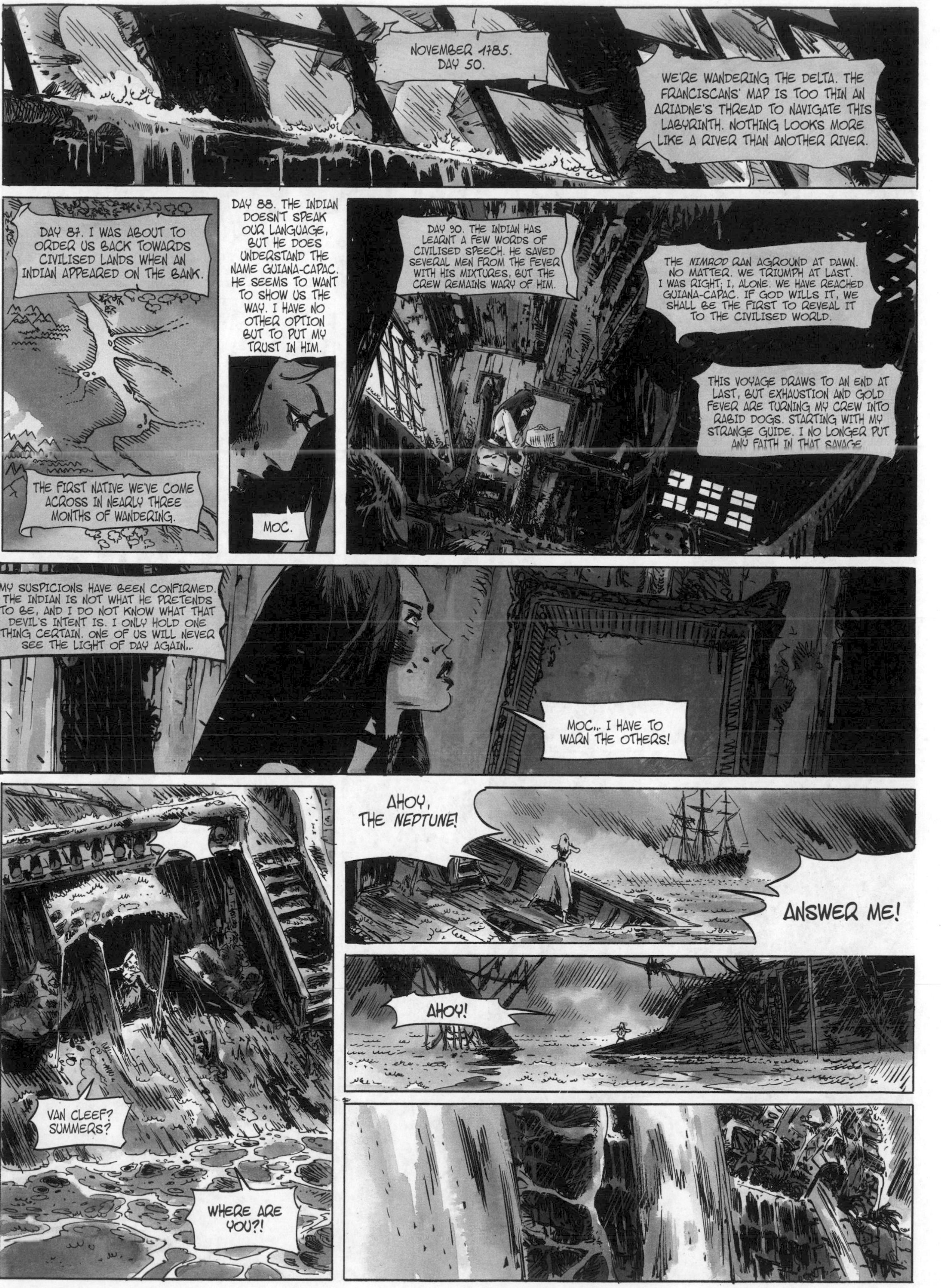

NOVEMBER 1785. DAY 50.
WE'RE WANDERING THE DELTA. THE FRANCISCANS' MAP IS TOO THIN AN ARIADNE'S THREAD TO NAVIGATE THIS LABYRINTH. NOTHING LOOKS MORE LIKE A RIVER THAN ANOTHER RIVER.
DAY 87. I WAS ABOUT TO ORDER US BACK TOWARDS CIVILISED LANDS WHEN AN INDIAN APPEARED ON THE BANK.
THE FIRST NATIVE WE'VE COME ACROSS IN NEARLY THREE MONTHS OF WANDERING.
DAY 88. THE INDIAN DOESN'T SPEAK OUR LANGUAGE, BUT HE DOES UNDERSTAND THE NAME GUIANA-CAPAC. HE SEEMS TO WANT TO SHOW US THE WAY. I HAVE NO OTHER OPTION BUT TO PUT MY TRUST IN HIM.
MOC.
DAY 90. THE INDIAN HAS LEARNT A FEW WORDS OF CIVILISED SPEECH. HE SAVED SEVERAL MEN FROM THE FEVER WITH HIS MIXTURES, BUT THE CREW REMAINS WARY OF HIM.
THE *NIMROD* RAN AGROUND AT DAWN. NO MATTER. WE TRIUMPH AT LAST. I WAS RIGHT; I, ALONE. WE HAVE REACHED GUIANA-CAPAC. IF GOD WILLS IT, WE SHALL BE THE FIRST TO REVEAL IT TO THE CIVILISED WORLD.
THIS VOYAGE DRAWS TO AN END AT LAST, BUT EXHAUSTION AND GOLD FEVER ARE TURNING MY CREW INTO RABID DOGS. STARTING WITH MY STRANGE GUIDE. I NO LONGER PUT ANY FAITH IN THAT SAVAGE.
MY SUSPICIONS HAVE BEEN CONFIRMED. THE INDIAN IS NOT WHAT HE PRETENDS TO BE, AND I DO NOT KNOW WHAT THAT DEVIL'S INTENT IS. I ONLY HOLD ONE THING CERTAIN. ONE OF US WILL NEVER SEE THE LIGHT OF DAY AGAIN...
MOC... I HAVE TO WARN THE OTHERS!
VAN CLEEF? SUMMERS?
WHERE ARE YOU?!
AHOY, THE *NEPTUNE*!
ANSWER ME!
AHOY!

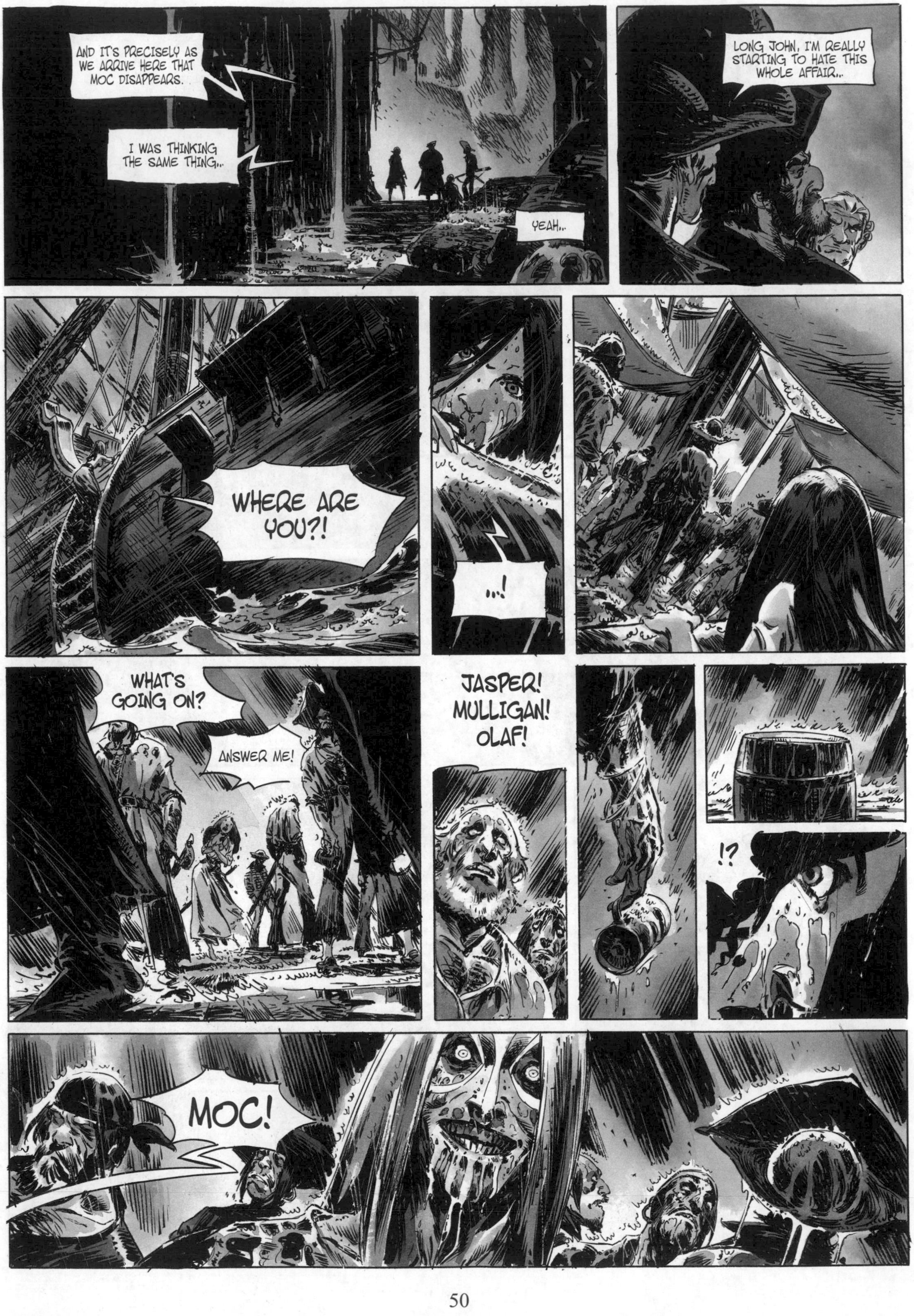

AND IT'S PRECISELY AS WE ARRIVE HERE THAT MOC DISAPPEARS.
I WAS THINKING THE SAME THING...
YEAH...
LONG JOHN, I'M REALLY STARTING TO HATE THIS WHOLE AFFAIR...
WHERE ARE YOU?!
...!
WHAT'S GOING ON?
ANSWER ME!
JASPER! MULLIGAN! OLAF!
!?
MOC!

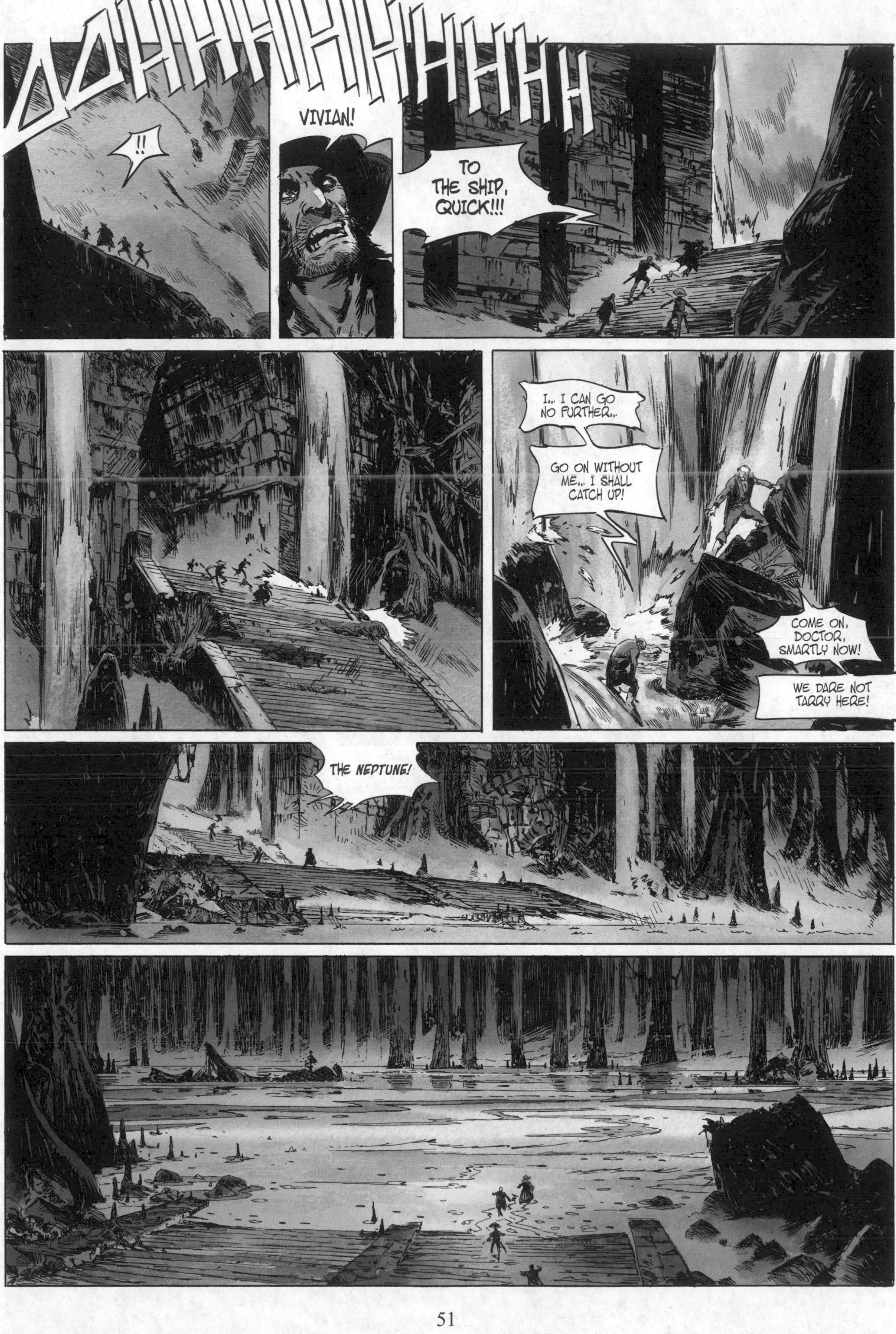
AOHHHHHHHHHH
!!
VIVIAN!
TO THE SHIP, QUICK!!!
I... I CAN GO NO FURTHER...
GO ON WITHOUT ME... I SHALL CATCH UP!
COME ON, DOCTOR, SMARTLY NOW!
WE DARE NOT TARRY HERE!
THE NEPTUNE!

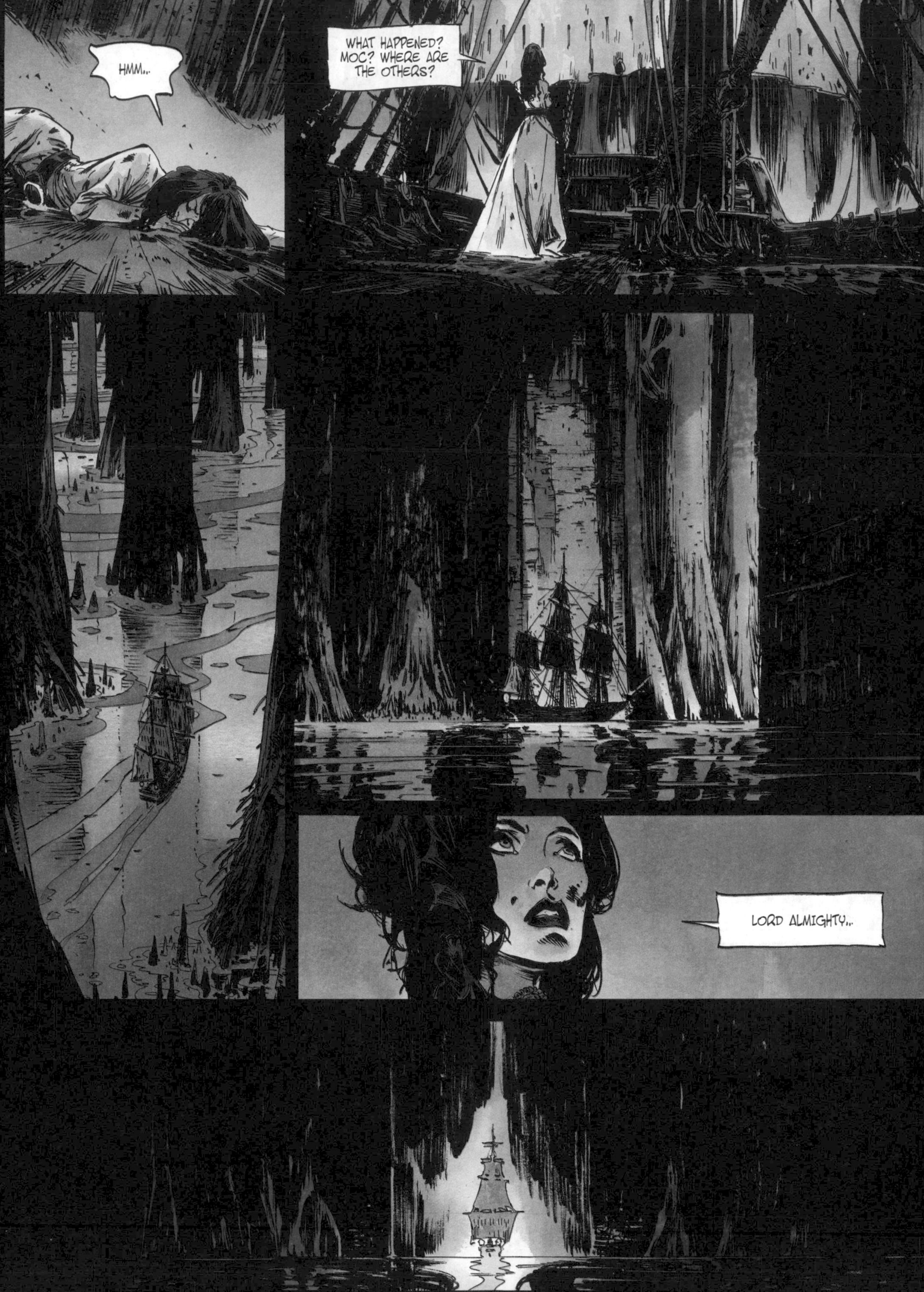
HMM...
WHAT HAPPENED? MOC? WHERE ARE THE OTHERS?
LORD ALMIGHTY...

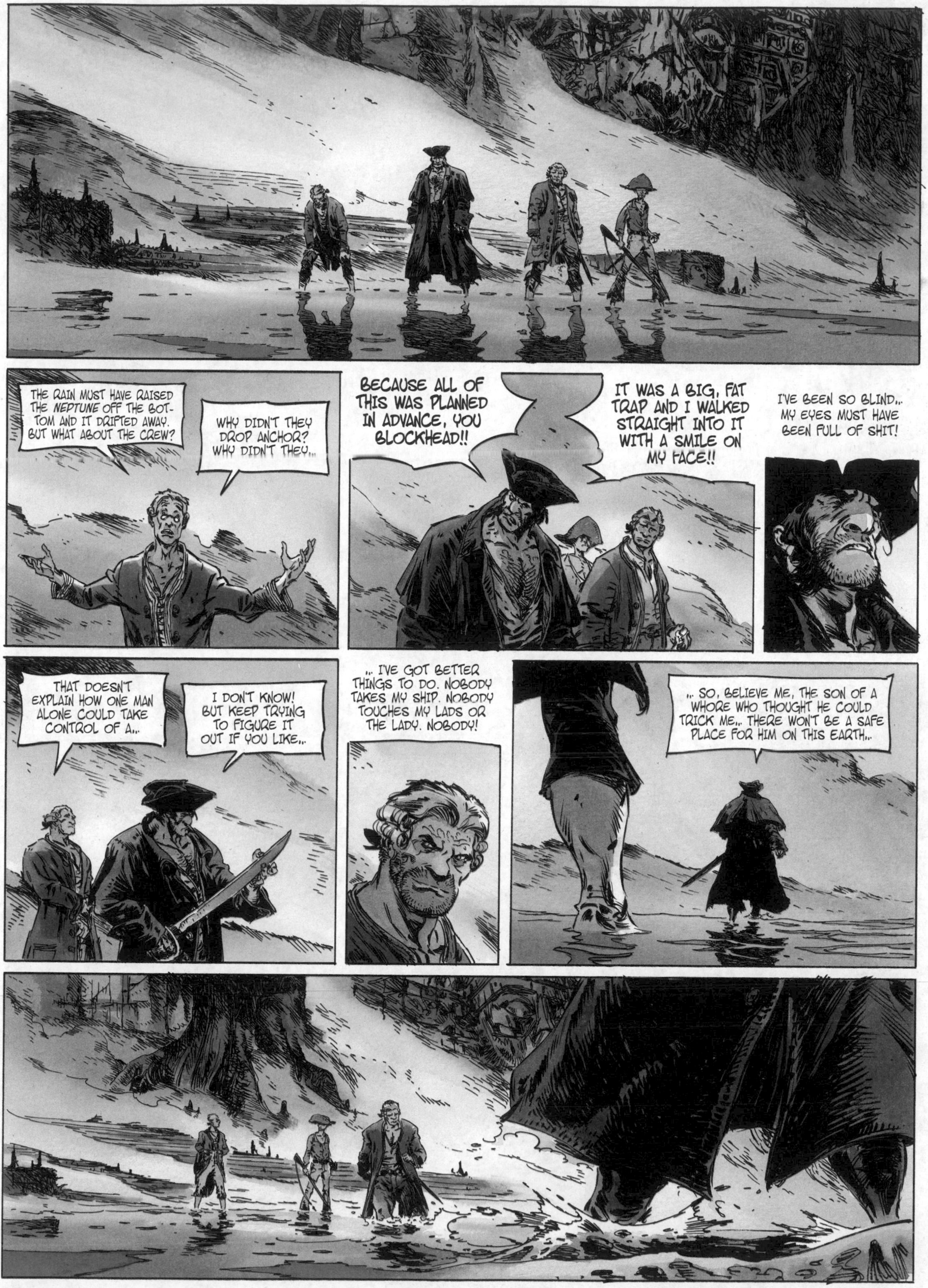
THE RAIN MUST HAVE RAISED THE *NEPTUNE* OFF THE BOTTOM AND IT DRIFTED AWAY. BUT WHAT ABOUT THE CREW?
WHY DIDN'T THEY DROP ANCHOR? WHY DIDN'T THEY...
BECAUSE ALL OF THIS WAS PLANNED IN ADVANCE, YOU BLOCKHEAD!!
IT WAS A BIG, FAT TRAP AND I WALKED STRAIGHT INTO IT WITH A SMILE ON MY FACE!!
I'VE BEEN SO BLIND... MY EYES MUST HAVE BEEN FULL OF SHIT!
THAT DOESN'T EXPLAIN HOW ONE MAN ALONE COULD TAKE CONTROL OF A...
I DON'T KNOW! BUT KEEP TRYING TO FIGURE IT OUT IF YOU LIKE...
... I'VE GOT BETTER THINGS TO DO. NOBODY TAKES MY SHIP. NOBODY TOUCHES MY LADS OR THE LADY. NOBODY!
... SO, BELIEVE ME, THE SON OF A WHORE WHO THOUGHT HE COULD TRICK ME... THERE WON'T BE A SAFE PLACE FOR HIM ON THIS EARTH...

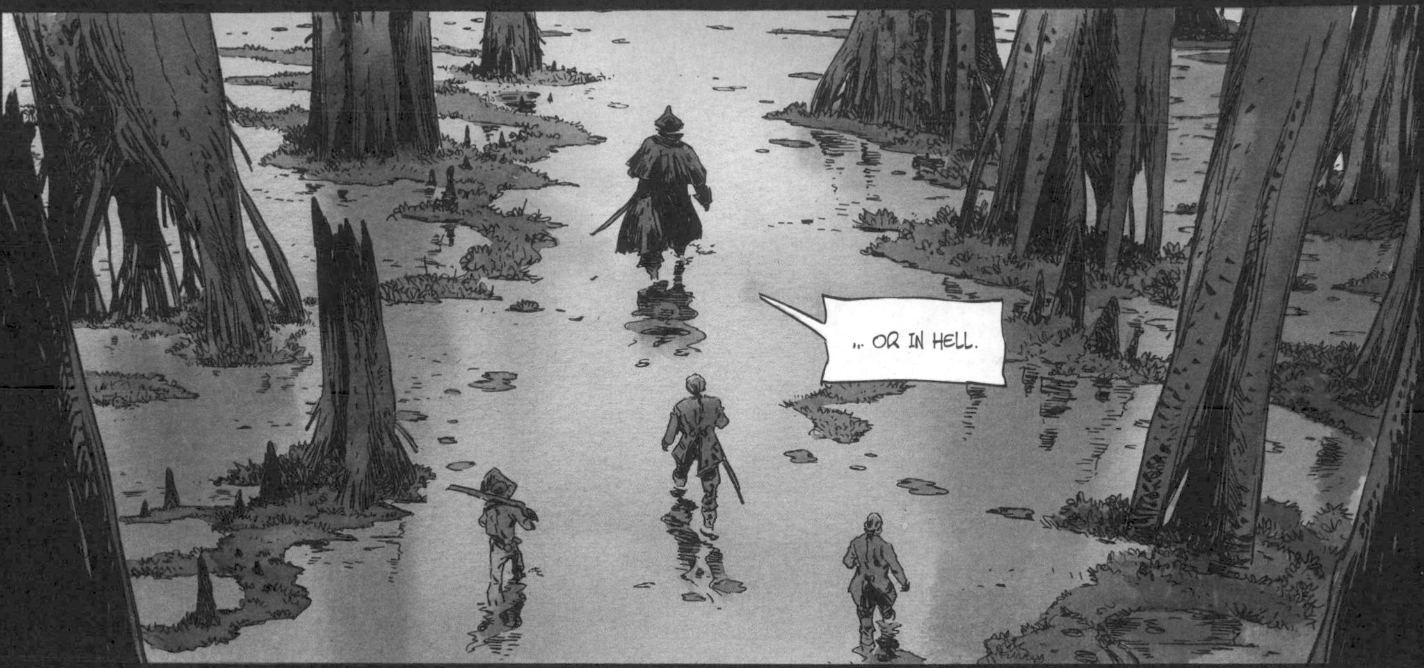
... OR IN HELL.

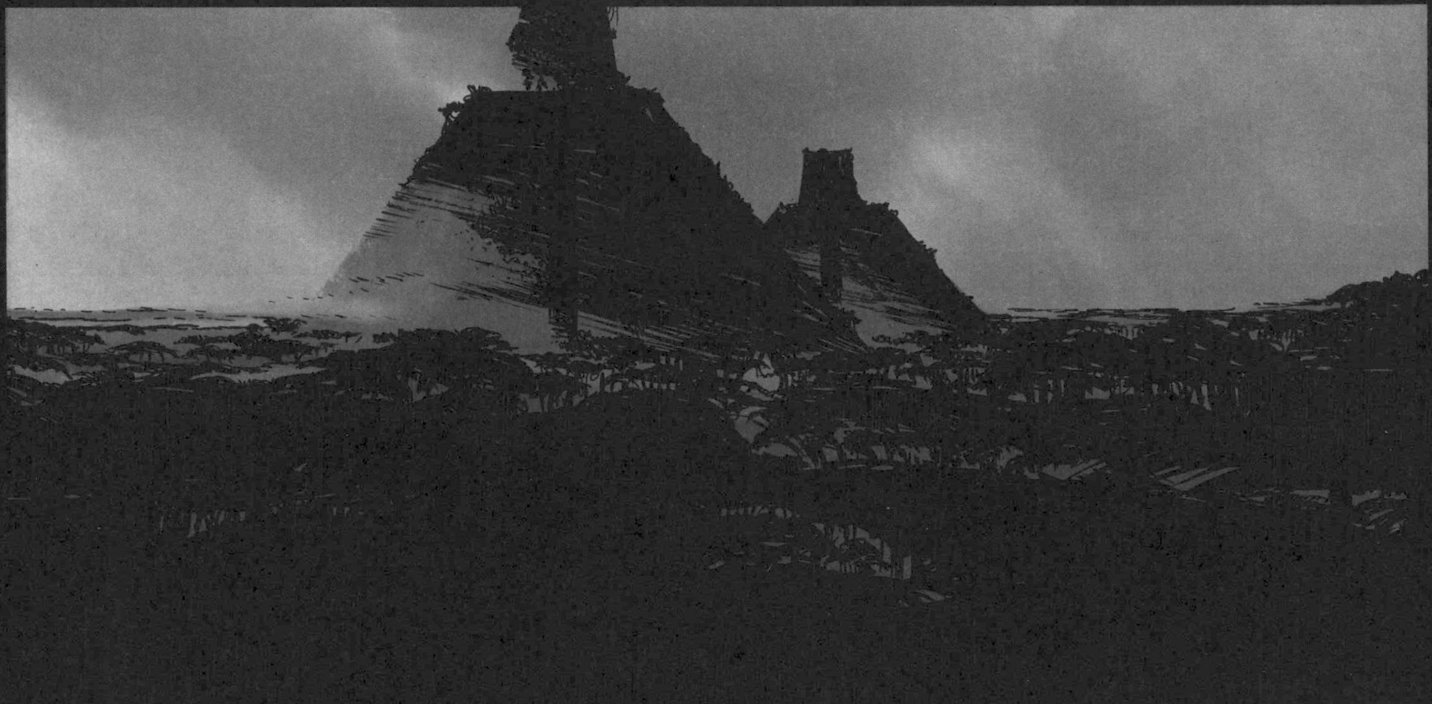

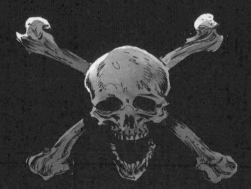

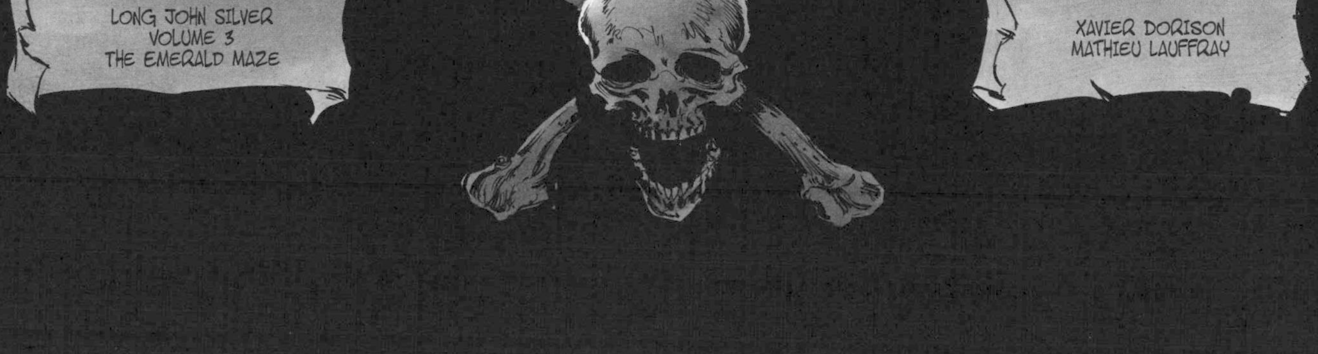
LONG JOHN SILVER
VOLUME 3
THE EMERALD MAZE
XAVIER DORISON
MATHIEU LAUFFRAY

THIS BOOK DOES NOT CLAIM TO BE A SEQUEL TO *TREASURE ISLAND*.
MERELY AN HOMAGE TO AN EXTRAORDINARY MASTERPIECE THAT HAS NEVER
STOPPED EVOKING WONDER IN US EVER SINCE WE WERE CHILDREN.
ITS ONE AND ONLY GOAL IS TO FIND AGAIN A BIT OF STARDUST FROM
THE GREAT DREAM THAT ROBERT LOUIS STEVENSON SPARKED…

XAVIER DORISON

MATHIEU LAUFFRAY

XAVIER DORISON IS ONE OF THE RISING STARS OF THE FRENCH COMIC SCENE. AUTHOR OF SEVERAL SUCCESSFUL SERIES SUCH AS "WEST," "SANCTUARY" AND "THE THIRD TESTAMENT," HE ALSO CO-WROTE THE SCRIPT OF THE FRENCH MOVIE "LES BRIGADES DU TIGRE."

MATHIEU LAUFFRAY DRAWS, AMONG OTHERS, THE SERIES "PROPHET." HE HAS WORKED AS A CONCEPT ARTIST FOR THE CINEMA ("BROTHERHOOD OF THE WOLF") AND VIDEO GAMES INDUSTRY ("ALONE IN THE DARK 4").

LONG JOHN SILVER

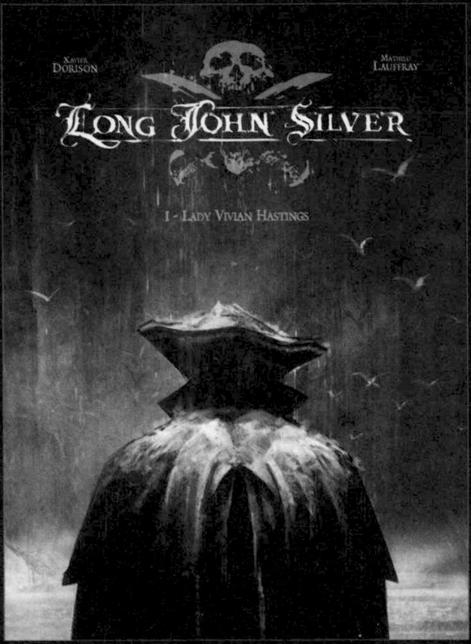
XAVIER DORISON
MATHIEU LAUFFRAY
LONG JOHN SILVER
I - LADY VIVIAN HASTINGS

I - Lady Vivian Hastings

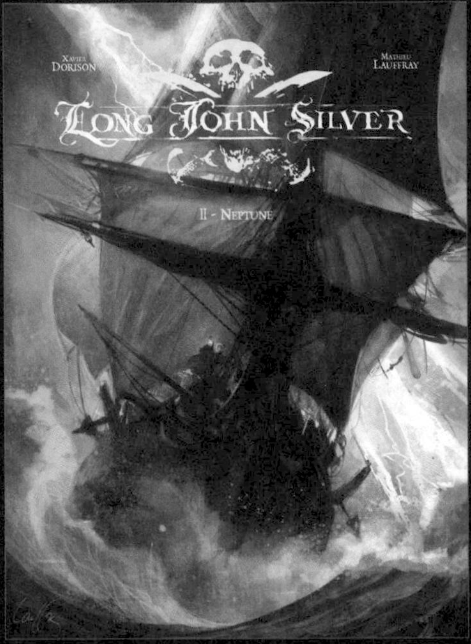
XAVIER DORISON
MATHIEU LAUFFRAY
LONG JOHN SILVER
II - NEPTUNE

II - Neptune

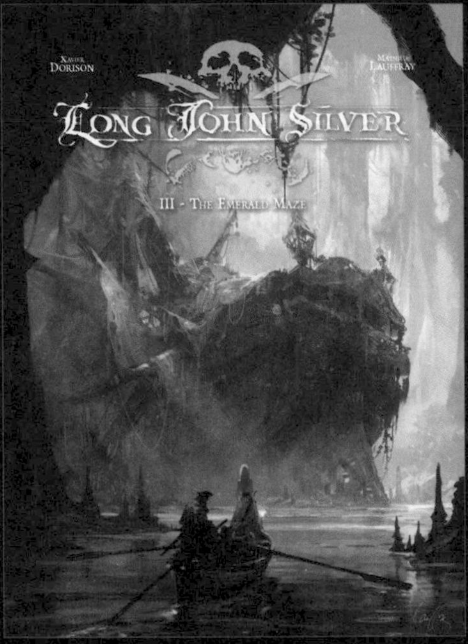
XAVIER DORISON
MATHIEU LAUFFRAY
LONG JOHN SILVER
III - THE EMERALD MAZE

III - The Emerald Maze

COMING SOON:
IV - Guiana-Capac